# Cashing In at the Checkout

# Cashing In at the Checkout

Susan J. Samtur
with Tad Tuleja

**The Stonesong Press**
a division of Grosset & Dunlap, Inc.
**New York**

*Designed by Joyce Schnaufer*

10 9 8 7 6 5 4 3 2 1

Library of Congress catalog card number: 79-51120

ISBN: 0-448-15704-7

# Contents

# Introduction.
# Getting Them
# to Pay You

In the spring of 1978 I sent NBC News a copy of my refunders' newsletter, *Refundle Bundle,* and asked if they
would be interested in doing a story on Supershopping,
the System I had developed to cut my grocery costs. Later,
on the phone, I told them about part of my System, couponing. They were impressed with the amount of money the
average shopper could save by a combination of judicious
planning and couponing, and decided to take me up on my
offer. Would I be interested in going on a shopping trip
with the producer of consumer expert Betty Furness's
show to demonstrate what kind of savings were possible?

Would I! "Fine," said NBC. "You pick the store, and
we'll send a camera crew to your house next Thursday."

Early the next Thursday morning, Rita Satz (the show's
producer), the camera crew, and I set out. We must have
made a strange picture trooping into the store, me with my
cart and batch of carefully selected coupons, Ms. Satz with
her microphone, and the crew winding around us like pilot
fish, with their wires, camera, and lights. I know that
plenty of heads turned, and I could see on more than one

1

shopper's face the question, "Now what kind of stunt is this?"

Stunt it may have been, but it proved its point. As my first cart filled up and the manager obligingly wheeled over another, I could see eyes going wide, and the crew began to look skeptical. I had taken only about $40 with me, and they knew it. Yet by the time I'd finished with the meat, dairy, and produce aisles and was starting in on cleansers, we all knew I had a lot more than $40 in merchandise.

When I finally wheeled the two overflowing carts up to the register, the checker looked at me as if I might be the Old Woman in the Shoe in disguise. But she dutifully rang up the items, grinning for the camera, until my purchases formed a pyramid almost as big as the "Special on Beets" display at the end of the aisle behind us. We all held our breath as she punched the subtotal and then the total keys.

"That's $130.18, please," she said politely.

The crew shifted nervously, thinking no doubt about the two $20 bills in my purse. I smiled and handed the checker my coupons.

She began to total them up, which seemed to take twice as long as it had taken to total the merchandise itself, and then subtracted the coupon total from the bill. When she saw what the new bill was, she gave me a big smile. I could hardly believe my eyes either. The trip had gone even better than I had hoped.

The new total was $7.07. I had just saved $123.11—or approximately 95 percent of my bill.

This rather dramatic episode highlights just one of the steps in the profitable Supershopping System I have developed out of sheer necessity. Before Supershopping, ever-increasing food prices had made grocery shopping nothing but frustration for me. "Can we really afford lamb this week?" I would ask myself over and over again. "Wouldn't ground beef do just as well?" No matter how carefully I bargain hunted, I still had to employ all kinds of budget-trimming devices just to come up with three meals a day for my family of four. This went on for month after budget-conscious month.

Then I discovered the System.

It was my friend Jenny who first introduced me to the System. Several years ago, one of the big cereal companies had introduced a new product, and I was complaining to Jenny about the scalping we were taking on it. She reached around and pulled a notebook down from a shelf.

"I think there's a refund on that right now," she said.

She flipped through the pages for a few seconds and then pointed.

"Here it is. A dollar back. Good until next July."

I was tempted to chuckle, because Jenny had a reputation as a bargain nut. She would go to the market with her pockets bulging with clippings, and tie up the checker for days while she hunted for the Pampers coupon or the store special on mayonnaise. I figured the "refund" book was just one more crazy—and not very profitable—gimmick.

I couldn't have been more wrong.

She passed me the notebook, and I leafed through it with growing amazement. In neatly arranged columns, there were listings of literally hundreds of manufacturers' refund offers, giving the brand names, the amounts of cash rebate offered, the expiration dates, and the dates she had sent the forms in.

"All these companies will send you money back for buying their stuff?" I asked.

She nodded. "A lot of them are introductory offers, to get you to try new products. But there are plenty of staples there, too. You clip your refund form, send it in with the labels they ask for, and in a month or so they send you the money."

She smiled a little sheepishly, as if she were embarrassed to admit how well she was doing on these deals. "You know, Sue," she confided, "I've reformed. No more trash bins in the pocket. I've got it organized now, and it's amazing how well that's paid off."

*"How* well?" I asked, still skeptical.

"Well," she said, "in the last year I must have gotten back $500 or $600 in refunds. That's not even counting discounts in the supermarket with coupons. You really ought to give it a try."

Why not? I thought. That week I sent in for what was to be my first dividend: a one dollar refund from Del Monte. Within six months I was hooked.

Had someone told me at that time that there was a simple shopping method that could transform me from a supermarket casualty into a supermarket whiz; if she had said that organized use of coupons could cut as much as 50 *percent* from my grocery bill *every week;* if she had predicted that I would, by becoming a refunder, make dozens of new friends and actually start a refunding newsletter of my own—I probably would have called it all pie in the sky and forgotten about it.

Yet all of this has happened. Since I started couponing and refunding casually five years ago, I have gradually developed my techniques into what I call my Supershopping System. Using that system, I not only save over *one-half* of our food bill annually, but I'm actually paid, by manufacturers, over $1,500 *per year* in cash refunds.

One year our refund money paid the entire heating bill for our house. The next year it sent us on a Florida vacation.

What is the Supershopping System?

Actually, anyone who has ever spent any time in a supermarket already knows something about the System. If you've ever clipped a coupon to get 25 cents off a can of coffee, or sent in two box tops and $1 to get your child some treat, you're already a novice couponer and refunder, and you've already realized some savings.

But unless you're one of the relatively small number of Supershopping addicts like me, you probably don't do this on a regular or systematic basis. And that can be costing you money. The difference between haphazardly clipping cents-off coupons and following my Supershopping System is the difference between a few pennies saved per week and envelopes full of dollars in your mailbox *every day.*

At a time when retail food prices are going up at the rate of nearly 10 percent a year, the American shopper needs all the help he or she can get. That is why I have written this book. It presents the System I've refined during the last five lucrative years, both for the already active refunder (there are over 50 million of you) and for the person who knows nothing at all about Supershopping. It's my belief that if you apply the principles outlined in this book, in a matter of weeks you will begin to reap financial rewards far beyond any you can now imagine.

Chapter 1 begins discussing some of the schemes shoppers have used to contend with the rapidly increasing grocery prices of the last few years. While many of these schemes have considerable merit, they share a common disadvantage: they rely on shopping styles and marketing outlets unfamiliar to the vast majority of American shoppers. For that reason, they are at the very least inconvenient. In the first chapter you will see how you can adopt Supershopping without making any radical changes in your current shopping habits.

The rest of the book explains how, by using Supershopping, you can cease being victimized by high food prices and become master of your food budget.

The first thing you must do to bring about this transformation is to become an alert, rather than a passive, shopper. In Chapter 2, I show you how to do this. I explain how the American supermarket is designed to get your last quarter, and how, by following the System, you can turn the tables on manufacturers and get *them* to pay *you* for shopping.

Chapter 3 discusses the food industry's most widely used—and most widely misunderstood—advertising gimmick, the coupon. You'll learn how those cents-off coupons can work for you instead of turning into confetti in your kitchen drawer. You'll see why it's wise to buy the "more expensive" nationally advertised brands, and why you should be willing to switch brands.

Chapter 4 deals with the real heart of my System: refunding. I'll tell you why saving every label and box top you have can be not only extremely profitable, but a lot of fun besides. This chapter explains such common refunders' terms as "qualifier," "proof of purchase," and "required blanks," and it shows you how to cash in on valuable offers with a minimum of time and effort. You'll find out how, for the past three years, the food companies have been paying me approximately $30 per week (that's cash on the barrelhead) for refunding. And I'll offer tips on the best ways to remove and store box tops and labels.

In Chapter 5, you'll be introduced to the rapidly growing refunding movement, and learn why there are now over fifty national newsletters devoted to saving you money. You'll see how subscribing to these inexpensive periodicals can drastically cut your food bill and introduce you to new friends through swapping coupons, refund offers, and forms.

Money is not the only reward for becoming a Supershopper. Chapter 6 discusses the many bonuses (the manufacturers call them "premiums") the alert shopper can receive in addition to cash rebates. In this chapter I'll show you how I acquired a slow cooker, half a dozen tee shirts, a child's wagon, and a barbecue set—all for the mere cost of postage.

Chapter 7 clears up some of the most common misconceptions about couponing and refunding—especially the false argument that it simply takes too much time.

Supershopping, I believe, is an idea whose time is long overdue. With it you can realize dramatic savings without dramatically changing your eating and shopping habits. Supershopping has taught me that I don't have to remain a victim of rising grocery prices; by using the food industry's own promotional devices, I've been able to come out ahead, in both time and money. Not only do I spend less time shopping than I did five years ago, but I do it at half the price.

Supershopping can help you to do this, too. There's no reason to succumb to panic or despair as manufacturers continue to up the ante on your groceries. With very little work you can, like me, get *them* to pay *you*.

# 1/Shopping Schemes and Dreams

Remember the old nickel Coke?

Chances are that, if you're over twenty-five, you do. It was only about two decades ago that a bottle of Coca-Cola cost you 5 cents. Today, the standard-size bottle will run you anywhere from 25 to 45 cents. I hate to guess what it will cost by the time my children are grown. I have visions of the major beverage companies dispensing soda to my grandchildren in eyedroppers, at a couple of dollars a shot.

The nickel Coke has gone the way of starched collars and high-button shoes, and it's been accompanied, sad to say, by such other symbols of a younger, less hectic America as the 15-cent Coney Island frank and even the 10-cent bag of French fries. The old advertising image of Mom and Dad feeding a hungry brood on two bucks flat now has the faded charm of a Civil War tintype: it's become impossible to buy a filling meal anywhere in the United States for much less than $1.50 per person, unless your family is composed of habitual dieters.

Since World War II, especially, food prices have been rising with alarming regularity. The increases have been

most drastic for restaurant and take-out food, but even for
people who have all their meals around the dining room
table, the cost of those meals has become a running joke.

## You Can Beat Inflation

Of course, inflation has cut into our paychecks on all sides:
it's not only food that's making us groan. But for me, at any
rate, the increases I see in the supermarket hurt more than
those on most other items because food is something so
immediate, so necessary on a daily basis, that I can't turn it
into an abstract or distant concept. You see the groceries
every day; when you put a jar of peanut butter on your shelf
and the label sneers, "A dollar nineteen, sucker," then you
know what inflation means.

Moreover, in recent years, food costs have been outstrip-
ping costs for other goods, and this means that the supermarket shopper feels the inflationary crunch with special
severity.

Look at the Consumer Price Index, for example. The CPI,
which is the government's official register of price fluctua-
tions, shows that between 1967 and 1972 the cost of food
rose slightly more slowly than the cost of all items measured as a whole. In 1973, this trend turned around and
every year since then the annual inflationary rate for food
has been *higher* than the rate for "all items" together.

In 1977, to be specific, the "all items" index was almost
182, measured against the 1967 base of 100. This means
that what you could buy in 1967 for $1, in 1977 cost you
$1.82.

That's bad enough. But the *food* index in 1977 was 194,
which meant that grocery prices in that ten-year span had
almost *doubled*. (The only 1977 item that topped the food
index was medical care.) And economists now say that our
economy has grown accustomed to about an average 10
percent rise on food each year.

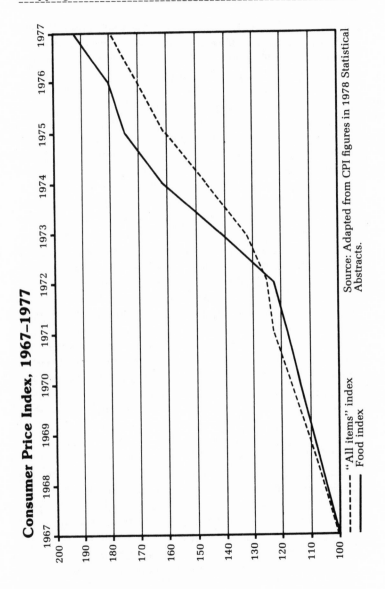

Figure 1: Consumer price index, 1967–77.

For certain food items, the inflationary rise has been even steeper. Margarine, for example, costs over twice as much as it did in 1967. Fish costs two and a half times as much. For a few months in 1977, coffee, that traditional staple of the American breakfast table, cost over four times as much! Since the average family spends 15 to 20 percent of its income on groceries, such inflated prices can have a serious overall effect on the family budget.

What can the shopper do about it? Assuming that the CPI will continue to inch upward at its "customary" 10 percent a year, is there any alternative to despair?

Actually, there is a great deal you can do. To confront the monster of galloping inflation, the American shopper has conjured up countless schemes and bargain tactics. I've tried many of these schemes myself, and in this chapter I want to talk a little bit about how I've found them all disappointing—at least when compared to Supershopping.

I know a lot of people swear by these schemes, and I think it's only fair to examine them first—to look at their merits as well as their defects—before describing my System. Once you understand how other schemes have proved of only limited use, you'll be in a better position to see what I mean when I say that Supershopping is easier, more fun, and more likely to save you big money.

## Skimping and Saving

By far the most common way that shoppers choose to deal with food inflation is, putting it bluntly, to go without.

You know the tactics employed: budget trims, bargain hunts, and general all-around belt tightening. Because you know you can't possibly pay both the grocer and the landlord, you decide to get by on less or lower quality food. If the dollar won't stretch, your stomach will just have to shrink.

So you pass by the top round and get the fattier ham-

burger meat. You zero in on damaged and therefore reduced merchandise. You buy day-old bread and cut out
everything that could possibly be considered a "frill," including most sweets and convenience foods. Before you
know it you've cut the grocery bill all right, but your family
thinks you're Lady Macbeth.

It's amazing the lengths to which grocery inflation can
force us. Hit by rising prices, shoppers have had to resort—
and are still resorting—to extraordinary ploys to keep their
bellies filled. A few years ago, for example, when the price
of beef tripled almost overnight, many supermarkets in the
New York area reported a rapid rise in the sale of canned
dog food. After a quick estimate of the canine population,
supermarket analysts concluded that Fido's dinner was in
many homes ending up not in his dish but on his master's
plate!

Or take our friends the Browns. Gloria's a school bus
driver and Bill's a teacher, which nets them a combined
salary barely sufficient for their needs. So they've been
turning into hard-core skimpers, almost evangelistic in
their devotion to the old Ben Franklin injunction "Waste
not, want not." Recently Bill came up with a casserole idea
that utilizes potato peelings. "Nutritious as hell," he
boasts, and no doubt he's right—but the taste is something
else again.

What Bill did on a small scale, a housewife named Jo
Ann York did on a larger one. In 1975 Mrs. York, a dedicated skimper, wrote a book called How I Feed My Family
on $16 a Week in which she outlined various ways to make
two meals out of the same amount of food she'd been accustomed to using for one. I have to admit she came up
with some excellent bargain recipes, but the bottom line,
which she was quick to acknowledge, was that the Yorks
simply got used to eating less. She had succeeded in ac-
complishing a small miracle, yes, but it involved a major
change in her family's eating habits.

Maybe you're willing to make that kind of change, and I

won't say you'd be mistaken in doing so. I guess we could all benefit from slightly smaller portions, fewer second helpings, and so on. But that doesn't mean we should be eating leftovers six times a week, and there's no guarantee that drastic skimping will make any of us healthier or happier people. In fact, there's the chance that cutting down on food, if carried too far, can damage health and happiness.

I've done my share of skimping, naturally. In this inflationary age, who hasn't? I can remember plenty of times when I've stretched a stew so thin that, as Woody Guthrie once put it, "even a politician could see through it." Before I got into Supershopping, in fact, I considered myself a local expert on ground beef; I think I must have tried forty or fifty exotic recipes that, when you actually bit into them, came out tasting remarkably like hamburger. I won't even begin to tell you disguises I invented for tuna casserole.

Finally, there was something ultimately dissatisfying about all my attempts to cut the budget as well as onions in the kitchen. It was, I guess, a simple matter of volume. The "politician's stew" might be great on your pocketbook, but it really doesn't fill your belly.

We are, after all, a nation of high-level consumers. We are used to a certain standard of living and a certain daily allotment of food. You can argue the moral or nutritional implications of high consumption as long as you like, but it won't alter the basic fact that Americans are accustomed to eating a lot, and eating well. Any scheme that aims to trim an American shopper's budget had better take that into account. I don't believe the "skimp-and-save" schemes do so.

It's my belief that saving is not the same thing as skimping. Sure, you can knock yourself out hunting for those half-price damaged cans, you can stretch a potato four ways, but if dinner becomes drab in the process, what's the payoff? Ardent skimpers are often fond of announcing that such and such a dinner cost only 14½ cents per person, and that's commendable, but not if nobody wants to eat it.

With my Supershopping System, as you will see, you can put extremely inexpensive meals on the table *without radically changing your eating habits.* This is the big advantage Supershopping has over skimping. I won't say my weekly menu is as cheap as seven days of spud peelings. I will say it's a lot tastier.

## Growing Your Own

The "back-to-the-land" movement of the 1960s gave a lot of young people the impression that if they would, as John Prine says, "blow up their TVs and eat a lot of peaches," their problems would soon disappear. Thousands of men and women, including entire families, climbed into vans and moved to the country to try their hands at farming, confident that if they couldn't get rich off the land, they'd at least be able to feed themselves and thus avoid the 60 percent markup they had been paying in supermarkets for food that had to be shipped, processed, and packaged after leaving the farm.

It was a great idea, but you know what happened to it. In the first season, most of the hopefuls discovered that farming was anything but the romantic idyll they had envisioned. It meant getting up at 5:00 A.M. with the cows, collecting eggs each afternoon, and chopping wood and hauling rocks and hoeing weeds for more hours each day than most of them had ever spent on anything else in their lives. Farming, it turned out, was hard work. Within a couple of seasons, the bulk of the latter-day pioneers were back in the cities and small towns, hankering for a Milky Way and some fries.

The "grow-your-own" movement has hung on, though, in more modest and sensible ways. With the dream of the

subsistence farm on the wane, the latest scheme has become the near-subsistence garden. A couple of years ago
*New York* magazine ran an article on gardening in the city,
showing terrace after terrace bulging with eggplants, tomatoes, and summer squash. It was amazing, the article
marveled, how much food you could grow in a small space.

True enough, but what if you don't happen to be one of
the lucky city dwellers that *has* a terrace? What if, like most
urbanites, you have barely room for a spice shelf, much less
rows of fresh herbs? You can use Grow-Lites, I guess, but
the amount of food you can grow under one of those things
wouldn't feed my family for a weekend. For the city apart-
ment dweller, growing your own can be a fantasy or a
hobby. It will not put much food on the table.

You're a little better off in suburbia. With, say, a quarter
acre of land, you probably could grow enough food in a
season to significantly save on shopping for the rest of the
year. Provided, of course, that you have a good-sized
freezer to store your produce—and that you're willing to
put in the many hours of daily attention that even the
smallest working garden requires.

My husband Steve and I took a fling at gardening a few
years ago, and very quickly discovered that, as a couple of
working stiffs, we really felt we had better things to do with
our evenings than break out the old rake and hoe. And if
you're not willing to devote some time almost every day to
tending your small plot, all you're going to harvest are potato bugs and ragweed.

What's the solution, then? Is there any way in which the
grow-your-own philosophy can work as an alternative to
pushing carts down the supermarket aisle?

Not, I'm afraid, on a small scale. There are exceptions,
naturally, but by and large the only people who successfully grow their own food are professional, full-time farmers. Not weekend gardeners or vegetable hobbyists, but the
bare 5 percent of the country's population that actually
lives and works on the land.

I'm not addressing this book primarily to them. If you're a farmer, Supershopping can still help you realize substantial savings on nonfood items (paper towels, cleansers, shampoos, dog food, and so on), but chances are even this System won't enable you to beat your own price for food.

If you're not a full-time farmer, however, Supershopping can show you how to pay almost as little for those beans or potatoes as those who have grown them for you.

## Assessing the Alternate Suppliers

The 1960s "alternate life-style" movement didn't stop at the farm. For every back-to-the-lander, there were dozens of people who chose slightly less exotic ways of battling the supermarkets' grip. Rather than cut out all middlemen by going directly to the land, these people cut out merely the most visible middleman, the supermarket itself, which (it was believed) was most responsible for high prices and falling quality.

This search for alternate suppliers has lasted in a way the grow-your-own movement has not, because it's a lot easier to change your market than your residence. Today, although the major supermarket chains have not been significantly hurt by them, there are numerous food co-ops, health-food stores, and farmers' markets throughout the country that cater to those who feel the big stores are out to do them in.

Are the alternate suppliers any better?

Food co-ops seem like a genuinely good idea. These are small stores where the clientele is composed of members, each of whom pays nominal annual dues for joining and in addition contributes a few hours of labor each month to keep the collective operation going. Because co-ops buy in bulk directly from the farms, they can offer their members fresh food daily, and usually at a slightly lower rate than even the big chain stores.

There's a catch, however, even if you're lucky enough to find one of these "people's stores" in your town. The catch is that selection is limited to what, in any one week, the co-op membership or its board decides are the best buys available. This means that, if cabbage is a steal this week but corn is high, you'll have to hold off on the corn fritters until the next shopping run. To be honest, co-ops do maintain a pretty decent selection most of the time, but you should realize that members may be obliged to plan their menus not simply around family preferences, but around the local growers' current sales.

Health-food stores usually carry a wider selection of items than co-ops, and are always well stocked with vitamins, nutrition books, and advice as well as food. Whether or not these places are a bargain is highly questionable. They do offer more "healthful" products than those available in your local supermarket—if you accept the notion that additives and preservatives are unhealthy. But can their goods be so much better for you that they are justified in charging the prices they do?

Like all small stores, health-food outlets must make up in unit price what they lose to the chains in volume. Sometimes this can mean incredible markups. On the stores' own brands, as well as on the fresh produce, it's impossible to determine what the markups are. But on goods that are available in the more conventional stores, loyal health-food shoppers take a drubbing indeed. I priced a package of tea in my local supermarket recently, and then compared it to the same package at the health-food store down the block. Same brand, same size—and a difference in price of 25 percent!

So if you shop in these places for your health, fine: may you live to be one hundred. But if you shop there with the notion that you are beating the supermarket system at the same time, forget it. When it comes to money, these places can only deepen the shopping blues.

Finally, there are farm stands, where the apples sit in baskets and Indian corn hangs on the trees. They are family owned and run, so that when you buy from them you are going to the grower direct.

Colorful and appealing as they are, however, few of them are as cheap as you would expect from places with little overhead, minimal labor costs, and no middlemen to contend with. I've found that they're a lot cheaper than the health-food places, and not much more expensive than the co-ops. But you pay for the privilege of using them. You pay in gas money, in time, and in convenience. How often, after all, can you afford to trek 10 miles down the road to stock up on fresh plums? And if, like so many city people, you don't own a car, these places are even more difficult to reach. In other words, farm stands are useful principally to mobile suburbanites.

We're pretty mobile, and I must admit we did consider using the roadside stands on a more regular basis when we were casting about for ways to battle the inflation goblin. There's no denying that it was fun to bundle up on a crisp November day and drive out to where the apples, even crisper, were displayed not in Saran Wrap but in colorful slat baskets. When the mood hits us, we still do it, as a lark. But not as a regular pattern. When we added up the gas and the tolls we spent on those country junkets, and then compared the prices of Farmer Radburn's apples with those in our local A & P, we realized we weren't coming out ahead by taking advantage of the grower-to-consumer situation. If you're driving by anyway, of course farm stands are a help. But you've got to live pretty close to the farm to make regular trips really pay.

In my view, the trouble with all the alternate suppliers is that, to profit from their use, you must be willing to adopt an alternate life-style—or at least significantly change your present shopping patterns. If you have a big freezer, you can still shop once a week; if you don't, you really should (like the Europeans) shop every couple of days to take full advantage of the freshness the alternate places offer. And that can cut into your time.

In addition, there are only certain things you can buy as an alternative shopper. You can forget about convenience foods. Buying only fresh produce means you will be spending your own time snapping those snap beans and slicing potatoes for French fries. If you don't mind the extra work, fine. If, like me, you're accustomed to popping the frozen beans in a pot and forgetting about them until they're done, then you may find the alternate supplier route a rockier road than you anticipated.

If you can do it, saving money by buying direct is wonderful. With Supershopping, though, you will not only save money but you'll also do it without having to go out of your way. You can buy in the same local supermarkets, buy the same name-brand products, but end up paying half as much.

## Why Store Brands Are Not Really Cheaper

So, we're right back in the supermarket aisle, flanked by endless rows of bold lettering and snappy pictures, all designed to convince you that This Brand, and no other, is best. Accepting that the supermarket, though it is surely no paradise, at least offers a wide choice and relatively fast service, you're faced with the common dilemma: Which brand, out of the mad array, offers the best buy for the money?

Many shoppers are loyal users of one or another national brand and buy that brand year after year, certain that they always know what they're getting. About 37 percent of American shoppers, according to a 1973 *Supermarket News* customer profile, buy exclusively brand-name items.

But just as many shoppers (another 37 percent) stick

with store brands, convinced that they're every bit as good as the national labels.

Which group is right?

Now, I can't tell you which brands to buy on the basis of which are "best." No studies have indicated that there is a very significant difference in "quality" between national and store brands, and I am frankly not impressed by people who swear that Birds Eye or Swanson or Kraft makes a "better" or "tastier" product than the competition.

Yet I buy brand names exclusively, and, in fact, a cornerstone of Supershopping is that you must buy only the nationally advertised brands, leaving the apparently cheaper store brands for the less systematic bargain hunters.

Why do I insist on this? The answer is simple: money. In the long run, *the brand name items are cheaper.*

Whenever I mention that Supershopping relies on brand-name shopping, I get incredulous stares. Somehow people won't believe that you can actually save more money buying the "expensive" brands than the bargain lines. On one radio show, a woman called in to say, "That's just not logical! Surely you'd save more by sticking with the cheaper items." Paradoxically, you wouldn't. Illogical as it may seem, the System reaps its greatest dividends only when you buy the "high-priced spread."

There's a simple explanation for this. Although the store brands may have cheaper price tags, they have the great disadvantage of being produced by companies who don't have the means to promote them. That means that 1) you cannot use coupons to buy them, 2) no one will ever offer you a refund for buying them, and 3) they are almost never on sale. The combination of these three factors means that, over the long run, you will lose out by staying with the bargains.

Say, for example, that you're pricing a canned vegetable. The Green Giant brand is going for 37 cents, while the same size in the store brand is only 32 cents. Most shoppers would consider the nickel-lower can to be a better value.

But not the Supershopper. She has checked through her coupons and come up with a 10-cents-off Green Giant coupon, which right away makes the nickel-higher item a nickel cheaper at the checkout. In addition, the Supershopper gets a Green Giant label from this sale, and in a few weeks that label, with others, may be worth another dollar in refund, so eventually she will have gotten the green beans free, and made 73 cents besides.

I don't have anything against store brands per se. There is a sameness about them, though, and if you like change as I do, the lack of innovative new products in the store-brand line can get to be aggravating. But I don't think there's a great difference in quality, and if I thought store brands were truly (rather than only apparently) cheaper, I'd probably switch to them myself.

According to a 1969 *Supermarket News* report, store brands average about 15 percent lower on ticket price than the nationally advertised brands. This seems like a big difference, but when you consider that I save approximately 50 percent on my grocery bill by sticking with brand names, it's not so big after all. Using the System leaves me a comfortable 35 percent margin for profit with coupons alone. Refunds add even more to my profits.

In addition, making money by buying the big companies' brands gives you, as any Supershopper will testify, a wonderfully satisfying feeling of having beaten the corporate giants at their own game. Sure, they'll still jack up the prices next week—and faster than the store brands—but they'll also offer a host of new coupons and refunds in compensation. With a little dedication to the System, you can learn to outguess them and turn each new increase into a dividend.

## Beating the Supermarket Blues

It looks as if price increases are with us for keeps. The reasons for this are debated constantly by everyone from the professional economist to the teen-age checkout clerk. But no one has yet come up with a clear, unshakable theory as to why the nickel Coke died.

Some blame the farmers. Others blame the markets. And still others point to the countless middlemen between. All of these take their cuts, of course, but the unkindest cut of all is taken by those who bear none of the responsibility and yet shoulder almost all of the burden of supermarket inflation: you and me, the consumers, victims of the supermarket blues.

National Productivity Commission official Roy Beasely summed up the situation well in a New York *Daily News* article written by Steve Lawrence on November 27, 1978. Speaking of the food industry, Beasely explained that "it grew up in an environment where all costs were just passed right on to the consumer. This is an industry that only knows one thing—how to increase prices."

Unfortunately, when it comes to food, the old law of supply and demand works only up to a point. Even the most dedicated skimper, confronted by outrageous prices, cannot simply stop eating in protest. Consumer boycotts taking this approach—the several meat boycotts of the last ten years, for example—have achieved at best only local and short-range victories.

My Supershopping System is unique in that, far from relying on alternative structures outside the general shopping patterns, it uses the food industry's *own* strategies as levers to loosen its grip. The tenets of Supershopping are neither complicated nor revolutionary. What they say, essentially, is that if you want to come out ahead at the checkout counter, you have to play the markets' own game—only play it better than they do. You can beat the system, but only if you use the ammunition it gives you.

In order to do this effectively, you must first know how the supermarket works. The American food industry operates as a game. The main difference between the supermarket game and most games of chance is that in the market the player is given a more than even chance of winning, if only he or she remains alert to what is going on. In the next chapter I'll show you how to do this.

## SUPERSHOPPING: A System Summary

If you're considering ways to save on your grocery bill, think about these facts before adopting a plan.

1. Food prices have been rising at an average of almost 10 percent a year. If you're tired of skimping and cutting corners on your food bill, Supershopping can show you how to stretch your food dollar without shrinking your stomach. This system will not require you to radically change your family's eating habits.

2. Alternate suppliers, growing your own, even buying the "cheaper" store brands are largely unsatisfactory ways to budget. Why? The alternates are low on selection, growing your own is financially impossible unless you're a farmer—and the store brands *aren't* cheaper in the light of Supershopping.

3. The Supershopping System can save you more money more easily than any other budget food scheme I've tried. Although it takes little time, space, or trouble, it can cut 50 percent off your grocery bill, every week.

# 2 / Winning the Supermarket Game

There's a rumor going around that supermarkets exist to sell food.

Actually, selling food is a secondary matter to them. The reason they exist is the same reason every other industry outlet exists: to make money. It's true that they do sell food in the process, but you shouldn't conclude from that that their purpose is a purely distributive one. Supermarkets do not stay in business by overseeing whether or not your pantry has enough crackers or cat food to meet your family's needs; they stay in business by getting you to spend money, and the more of it the better.

Supermarkets don't do this out of malice or contempt for the consumer. On the contrary, most supermarkets maintain a quite healthy respect for their customers, and are more than willing to steer you toward their cheaper and more convenient products. But this does not mean you should confuse them with philanthropic organizations. No store manager in his right mind is going to offer you a bargain that does not also show a healthy profit for the store.

# Shopping: A Game You Can Win

Supermarkets are like huge casinos, matching their wits and luck against each other to see which one will reap the lion's share of profits. The store that comes in first in this race is the one that succeeds in getting the most shoppers to spend the most money in the smallest amount of time.

Now, I realize there are some major distinctions between casinos and supermarkets. For one thing, there is an immediate tangible consolation for those who prefer to put their money down at the checkout counter rather than on the blackjack table: the groceries they come away with. Even if you've just dropped half your paycheck in the till, you do go home with those cookies and asparagus tips.

There is another major difference between casino games and the supermarket game. In all casino games, there is a mathematical certainty that, over the short as well as the long run, the house will win and the player will lose. In other words, the odds are always stacked against you in a casino. If you figure out a way to beat those odds—if you come up with a system to beat their system—they simply ban you from further play.

This is not the case in the supermarket. There is no mathematical certainty attached to any one marketing technique meant to make you buy; as a result, you can't say that the odds are stacked against you. In fact, the markets give you plenty of opportunity to manipulate the odds in a way that would just get you thrown out of games in Las Vegas. Unfortunately, very few shoppers take advantage of them.

Furthermore, the supermarket house rules do not bar the introduction of a system. If, as I have done, you come up with a system of beating the house every time, they still do not ask you to leave. I can't imagine an Atlantic City or Las Vegas casino doing anything at all for the customer whose intention is to beat the house. Supermarkets, on the other hand, almost beg you to hit bingo whenever you shop, and the Alert Shopper, using my System, can hardly fail to do so.

Alert Shoppers know the house rules and how to use them to their advantage, while Normal Shoppers fall easy prey to these very rules—because they're unaware of the supermarketing techniques designed to make them leave the store with dozens of things they hadn't thought they wanted. If you've ever come home with six cans of tomato paste instead of four simply because three were "on sale" for an odd-number price, you'll recognize what I mean.

Systems to beat the casino moguls come and go. Super-shopping, I believe, is here to stay. If you have any doubt as to whether it's high time it arrived, look at what happens to the Normal Shopper playing the supermarket game.

# How the "Normal Shopper" Loses the Game

In April 1978, the U.S. government publication *National Food Review* observed that "the 'careful shopper' [the individual who plans in advance, checks weekly specials, compares prices, and checks labels] is not the most prevalent in the marketplace."

If you've ever watched the way most of us shoppers scurry up and down supermarket aisles, snatching and plucking with barely a glance at the products we're acquiring, you might well agree with me that the "careful shopper" is probably the figment of some hopeful consumerist's imagination: a hypothetical being that has yet to make an appearance on this planet.

Sure, there are always a few odd ducks blocking traffic to look at labels, but if you watch them closely you'll notice that somewhere along the line—usually between the Pringles display and the end-of-aisle special on peaches—even these rare birds pick up a couple of obvious "impulse" buys. (This speculation is based on the assumption that no middle-aged label reader in her right mind would actually *plan* to buy three kumquats or a sample bottle of Farrah Fawcett shampoo.)

Now, it's pretty hard to measure the habits of the Normal Shopper, or to determine how many of us "plan in advance, check weekly specials," and so on. But we do have a little information on shopping patterns, collected by various government and industry surveys, and it gives you some idea of why most shoppers lose in the cart-pushers' game.

The *National Food Review* article quoted above, for example, hazards the guess that "shopping once a week seems to be firmly entrenched in the American life-style," and a 1972 *Supermarket News* survey bears this out. Over 50 percent of American shoppers, it found, shop regularly once a week—with nearly 25 percent shopping only twice, and only 6 percent willing to trek down the aisles more than three times a week.

The time spent on that once-weekly trip, moreover, is (according to *NFR*) generally a little under an hour; that should give you a hint both about how much shoppers look forward to the weekly chore, and about how careful they are in completing it.

You *can* shop successfully for a family in fifty minutes. I've done it many times. But it takes some prior preparation if you're not going to get stuck with thirteen bottles of on-sale soda and no main course. And this kind of prior preparation, to borrow the subdued phrase of *National Food Review*, is "not prevalent in the marketplace."

Economist Jennifer Cross, for example, states in her fascinating book *The Supermarket Trap* that 60 percent of the shoppers in the United States shop without a list. Think of what that implies about the Normal Shopper's habits. It suggests that most of us are used to walking into the supermarket pretty much unprepared. We may have a mental list but you know how easily that kind of list can be added to by impulse.

Lacking prior preparation, the Normal Shopper has no recourse but to buy on impulse and according to memory. That impulse may take thirty seconds or it may take three, but unless the shopper has a phenomenal memory, the decisions she makes in the aisle will bear only a sketchy relation to the gaps on her shelves at home.

So, the first way in which Normal Shopping plays into the house's hand is that it allows impulse rather than plan to guide the choice of purchases.

## When to Forget Loyalty

What other ways do we go out of our way to lose the game? For one thing, we practice a strange type of "loyalty," both to our favorite stores and to individual products within those stores.

According to the *Supermarket News* customer profile quoted before, 65 percent of American shoppers are considered "loyal" customers; that is, they do almost all of their shopping, week after week, at the same store.

In the era of the mom-and-pop store, store loyalty probably had a lot to do with friendship and real community feeling. In the age of the chain store, I can't see that it has to do with anything else but habit. Not only is this habit anachronistic, but it can be extremely hazardous to your budget. Suppose the A & P down the street is running a special on hot dogs. Does it really make sense for you to pay 30 or 40 cents extra per pound simply because that A & P is not "your" store?

Loyalty in the abstract is an admirable quality, but loyalty toward a giant chain can very quickly turn into the love of being enchained. If you can't bring yourself to switch stores to take advantage of sales two blocks away, you are stacking the odds against yourself. The minuscule amount of time you may save shopping a bit closer to home will hardly be worth adding a 15 or 20 percent surcharge to your shopping bill.

We all have our favorite markets, of course. For years I've patronized a major chain store near my home. But if I see an attractive special advertised by a rival store, I become Benedict Arnold in a minute. Being on the lookout for which store is offering you the best odds this week is an essential part of my Supershopping System. No food store is out to do you any favors. You may have a friend in a produce manager here or in a butcher there, but each store as a whole should be judged on precisely those merits which the stores themselves consider central: the quality of the merchandise and the price being asked for it.

Remember that one of the delightful things about playing "market roulette" is that, if you don't like a store's odds, you can take your business elsewhere. In the casinos, all the roulette wheels are alike, but supermarkets vary widely, because they are part of a competitive free market system. Check out the competition. It keeps them on their toes, and you'll thank yourself for comparing.

The same thing goes for *product* loyalty. Again, most of us seem to have our favorite brands, and another unfortunate aspect of Normal Shopping is that we often stick with those brands no matter how the prices soar. Brand-name "loyalty" makes no more sense to a Supershopper than loyalty to a particular store.

Look at the labels and you'll see that I'm right. The difference between one brand-name soap and another in terms of ingredients is often negligible, and since the big manufacturers should have no greater hold on your heartstrings than the big chains, why not buy what is cheapest? (The cheapest *brand* name, that is. Remember the discussion in Chapter 1 about store brands versus the nationals.)

Given the habits mentioned above, the Normal Shopper is sure to lose the shopping game. She sticks with one store, one line of products, and fills her cart with high markup items because she hasn't prepared ahead of time.

Are you a Normal Shopper? I know I was until I discovered the System. What the System taught me was that I could take matters into my own hands. I could shop not impulsively but _rationally_. And I could win at their game.

"The food industry," says economist Cross in her book, "does not want women to shop rationally." How right she is. But then she goes on to suggest that "to shop rationally, the housewife would need the impulses of a sleuth, the stamina of a weight lifter, and the skill of a certified public accountant." And there, I think, she is wrong. To shop rationally, you really need none of these things.

What you do need is a System based on an understanding of how supermarketing works from the seller's point of view. To help that understanding, I want to give you a few of his unwritten rules.

This in itself will not insure that you will be able to beat the seller's game. For that you'll need all the interlocking parts of my System. But it will give you a clearer idea about why you should be mildly suspicious as you shop, and it will tell you some of the methods the supermarkets use across the country to keep shopping odds in their favor.

## How the Major Food Companies Vie for Your Attention

Can you tell what Maxwell House coffee, Tang, Kool-Aid, Minute Rice, Log Cabin syrups, Birds Eye frozen peas, Post Grape Nuts, and Jell-O have in common?

They are all produced by the same company, the General Foods Corporation. This illustrates a basic element of the modern food marketing system: extensive diversification under a few giant corporate umbrellas. The days of the small local company are fading fast. Today, nearly everything on your shelf has been made by one or another firm that figures someplace in the Fortune 500. (General Foods, for example, is number 40. Campbell's Soups is number 143. Procter & Gamble, which makes Pringles and Duncan Hines cakes as well as soap, is number 20.)

This means that food has become big business. "Agribusiness," the experts call it, giving an official linguistic stamp to what has been common knowledge for decades. Most of our groceries are produced by a few gigantic concerns, and virtually every one of them spends millions of dollars each year to convince you and me that their products are superior to all others.

## Advertising

In 1976, for example, the biggest moneymaker of "household aids," Procter and Gamble, spent $360 million advertising its wares. In that same period, the big three automobile manufacturers spent only $70 million more *combined!*

Food advertising is enormous and constantly growing. Jennifer Cross estimates in her book that it supports between one-sixth and one-seventh of the nation's advertising agencies—not counting the food giants' own promotional departments. In 1977, the industry as a whole spent approximately $4 *billion* to get its products on your shelves.

What does that mean to you? It means that somebody out there wants your dimes and nickels very badly. And it means that they are willing to pull out all the stops to get them.

This is a mixed blessing for the shopper. On the one hand, the intensive competition for your shopping dollar may tend to keep inflation in check by leading to price wars, special promotions, and the like. On the other hand, the enormous expense of making sure you remember Product X's name must be made up for somewhere, and generally that "somewhere" is in the price you pay for the product, as advertising costs are simply passed on to the consumer. Costs of advertising and packaging—which today is a special kind of advertising—now account for a very high percentage of the price of our groceries. This is item one to remember when you consider the supermarket game.

## New products

Item two is the fact that manufacturers believe that, in order to keep your attention from month to month, they have to offer you a constantly changing array of new products. "Most businessmen and economists," according to Cross, "are hooked on the belief that an enterprise must grow, or die. . . . the ability to push successful new products is a *sine qua non* of this growth process."

It's nice, of course, to have a new cereal to try each month, but again the result for the consumer is mixed. Not only does the high cost of bringing out all those new cereals get passed on to us, but the proliferation of new products pushes manufacturers to subject you to saturation advertising and gimmickry in order to offset the sheer volume of choice. If there are only three coffees to choose from, advertising is a relatively simple matter. When the number of choices goes up to five or ten, extremely subtle ways must be devised to capture your attention.

Today's shopping choices are mind-boggling indeed. According to the A. C. Nielsen survey people, between 1964 and 1970 the number of items in the typical American supermarket went from an average of three thousand to an average of eight thousand. And the number is swelling all the time. In 1977 alone, Nielsen reported, approximately twenty-four hundred new products were dangled before the cart pusher's eye.

## In-store promotions

Most new products do just what most new businesses do: they never get off the ground. Only about 15 percent of them, in fact, ever make it into the second year's sales reports. As a result of this drastic attrition rate, manufacturers will do almost anything to get you to try a new item, and to keep on using it. In the markets themselves, store managers do their part to see that you remain convinced, and as an Alert Shopper you should be particularly wary of the techniques retail stores employ to promote new (and old) products.

Many store owners have learned a whole bag of psychological gimmicks to promote sales. By cagily arranging their floor plans, by promising big bargains, by using various pricing techniques, they are able to boost sales significantly. These techniques, employed by virtually every chain store in the country, comprise the way that the supermarket game is played from the companies' side. If you are unaware of them, they can take as big a bite out of your paycheck as the national TV ads by influencing you to buy unwanted products. If, as an Alert Shopper, you recognize them where they occur, you'll find they can become one of the most fascinating parts of the game to outwit. For a lively description of these techniques, see Steve Lawrence's "The Tricks of the Trade" in Nutrition Action, July 1976. The following discussion is based partly on that article.

## Marketing Techniques to Recognize

First of all, there are displays. In any one week your local market will very likely be featuring sales, specials, and display presentations of dozens of old and new items. A new soap powder will lure you with an "introductory" or "get-acquainted" offer, while an old one next to it displays a proud "5-cents-off" tag. At the end of one aisle a pyramid of tuna fish cans beckons you with a giant "Special" sign, while around the corner tomatoes are offered, prepacked, at "five for so-many cents."

The important thing to remember about all these inducements to buy is that a "sale" is not always a sale.

Many items that seem to be on sale actually have only been displayed to look like bargains. Don't be deceived by those huge, end-of-aisle pyramids. Often the items being pushed there are duds—things the store has had trouble moving off the shelves. Or they are high-profit items—things like crackers, light bulbs, and beer—that the management understandably wants to move quickly. The implication of "bargain" is there often when the items displayed are being sold at the normal price.

So check the prices and signs. Unless the display actually identifies itself as a sale display, chances are the "feature of the week" is last week's "dud of the week."

There are, of course, bona fide sales going on all the time, but the Normal Shopper seldom distinguishes between these and the flashy nonsales. One good way to determine which is which is to check your local paper for advertised sales. Generally the Wednesday, Thursday, and Sunday papers are full of advertised specials, complete with coupons to clip. By sticking with these, you can be sure your bargain is actually a bargain.

Supermarket *design* is another area in which market managers have become expert at getting us to buy. Although markets are ostensibly laid out along the lines of shopping convenience, what the manager considers when he is deciding to put the rutabagas next to the cheese dip or at the end of the soda aisle is an elementary salesman's question: "How can I get my customers to see the greatest number of products in the shortest time?"

With thousands of new items coming onto the shelves every year, store owners obviously can't expect to have their customers see everything. So they do the next best thing. They arrange the stores so the shopper must at least pass through every section before leaving. The reason the dairy department is so often at the rear of the store, for example, is because it has what market people call "drawing power." It acts as a magnet because practically everyone

needs to buy milk and eggs; as you head for this department, you pass numerous other items on the way.

"To do a normal shopping," New York's consumer affairs official Howard Tisch told writer Steve Lawrence,
"you have to go through every department in the store. The
shopper is forced to do exactly what the market people
want—hit all the high-profit items."

High-profit items, moreover, are often placed in the first
aisle, which you "hit" when you are still financially flush,
and near the registers, where you are a captive audience.
Produce, for example, is both a high-profit and a high-im-
pulse item. It's no accident that it's often placed in aisle
one. Nor is it accidental that candy and gum are stocked at
the checkout counter, where they will be all but irresistible
to a shopper waiting in line with a whining child.

Even within individual aisles, you're running a barrage
of subtle persuasions of which the Normal Shopper is unaware. Placement of articles on the shelves, for example, is
done with an expert knowledge of shoppers' scanning habits. Numerous studies have shown that items placed at *eye
level* sell faster than those on higher or lower shelves. The
items that the stores place there, as a result, are almost always high-profit impulse items.

The lesson here is that, if you're looking to cut fat off
your bill, you should spend the small extra effort it takes to
scan the lower and upper shelves. Consumer advocate
Adeline Shell, author of *Supermarket Counter Power*, told
Lawrence, "By looking up and down from eye level you
can save 10 percent or more depending on the store."

*Pricing*, too, is worked out to make you think you are
getting bargains even when you are not. Because the market experts have discovered that odd-cent prices are somehow mystically more attractive to shoppers than even-cent
prices, you'll seldom find a can of vegetables going for 38
or 40 cents; it's usually the magical 39.

To the Normal Shopper, presumably, that translates as a
bargain, whereas 38 would be somehow suspect. I must

confess I don't quite comprehend the subtleties of this technique. To a Supershopper, a penny is a penny is a penny.

Multiple-unit pricing is another retailing technique designed to convince the unwary that they're getting away cheaply when they're not. Whenever you see a "two-for" or "five-for" sign, be on guard. Again, the implication of "sale" is very strong, but if you check the prices of three single cans of beans against the "three-for" price, you'll very often find that the package deal is no saving. Store owners price items as triplets and twins because they haven't been able to move them singly.

By using all these techniques, the supermarkets are playing the game the way they know best, and it's no secret that when we buy more, they profit. I like to look at all these techniques not as inescapable traps but as opportunities for gaining a greater awareness of what skills you need to be an Alert Shopper.

Above all, I hope hearing something about these common techniques will put you on your guard, even make you a little suspicious the next time you enter a supermarket. Nobody says you have to beg them to take more of your money. With a little observation, you will see how the supermarkets, in the honest pursuit of profits, manipulate their customers' responses, and how, by becoming aware of that manipulation, you can turn it to your own advantage.

# STEP ONE: Learning the Rules of the Game

In this chapter I've described some of the ways in which you can lose in the supermarket game if you are not wary. Becoming alert to how that game works, then, is the first thing you can do in your own behalf. It's Step One in the Supershopping System. That in itself will not cut your food bill drastically, but it's an essential first step toward winning the game. "Consumers can save money at the supermarket," says author Lawrence, "but you do have to know the rules and pay attention."

You should now have some idea of the rules. It's up to you to pay attention. To summarize, here are some of the things you, as a budding Supershopper, should keep in mind:

1. Make a list and stick to it.
   I don't mean slavishly, but within reason. The shopper who has no idea what he or she is looking for is going to go home with a cartload of "unexpecteds."

2. Check the sales.
   Get the midweek and Sunday papers, and prepare yourself for that weekly shopping junket before going through the swinging doors. Clip and save the papers' coupons. Carry them with you when you go. Don't be afraid to switch brands or stores for the best prices.

3. Be cautious.
   A bargain is not always a bargain, even if an item is featured in a splashy end-of-aisle display. Check the prices and signs.

4. Shop with your eyes open.
   Compare prices, scan the shelves up and down as well as across, and realize that, no matter what pricing gimmicks are used, you have the final word.

# 3/Coupon Power

How many times have you opened a box of cereal and thrown away a 25-cents-off coupon offer inside because you figured it was "just too much trouble keeping track of those things?"

How many times have you ignored your local market's weekly flyer because you thought it wasn't worth it to clip coupons just to save a few cents on your bill?

How many times have you saved a cents-off coupon for months, then handed it to the checker only to discover it's expired?

If you're like I was before I developed the Supershopping System, you've done all of these things many times. American shoppers, bargain-conscious as they have had to become in recent years, still have barely scratched the surface when it comes to saving with coupons. Perhaps they think there is something slightly shameful or "cheap" about using these manufacturers dividends, or that using them is just another form of skimping. One common image of the dedicated coupon clipper, I suppose, is that of the slightly batty shopper who ties up the checkout line for an hour rummaging through twenty pounds of paper in her pockets. Coupon clippers seem to be thought of as a bit eccentric—as if there were something crazy about taking your savings seriously.

As a result, although almost 80 percent of American shoppers do use coupons from time to time, few of them do it in an organized way. In fact, less than one out of every ten coupons issued by the companies is ever redeemed at a store! This means that a lot of coupons—nearly 60 billion of them in 1977, in fact—are ending up in the trash.

That's just like throwing away money. If shopping can be considered a game, then coupons are truly "winner's chips." In this chapter, which outlines Step Two of my System, I'll show you why. If you believe for a minute that clipping coupons is a waste of time, think back to the shopping trip I took for NBC's Betty Furness.

## Shopping for Betty Furness

In the introduction to this book, I told about my shopping trip taken for the Betty Furness show. That trip netted a 95 percent savings on the total grocery bill—a phenomenal final bill of $7.07, instead of $130.18, after all the deductions were made for coupons.

At the time I agreed to do the show, I had been coupon clipping for years, and I had no worries that the trip wouldn't be a success in terms of savings. But the idea of being on national television really threw me. I couldn't just jump into the store unprepared; I'd have to plan, to get organized, to know what coupons I had and what I intended to buy before the news people arrived.

So I went to my "coupon file." This is simply a long, bulky envelope in which I keep, in alphabetical order, all the clipped coupons I now have on hand including cents-off coupons and free coupons from manufacturers. Before every shopping trip, I flip through them to see what items on my list I can get for a reduced price.

The flipping-through process took a little longer than

usual this time, because I was aware that my System was, in a sense, on trial, and I wanted to be sure that the savings I realized at the checkout would be truly spectacular. All in all, I think I picked out about fifty to sixty coupons—far more than I would have brought with me for a normal weekly shopping trip. But this was something special.

Then I checked through the local papers until I found a store in the area that fulfilled two requirements: 1) It had to be advertising a fair number of good sales and 2) it had to be featuring "doubling."

Doubling is a practice that is quite common in areas of intense competition. What it means is that the store will give you *twice* the value of your coupons instead of the face value. Thus, a 25-cent coupon is actually worth 50 cents, and a 50-cent coupon, one dollar. Stores do this to entice you into using them rather than the competition, and the practice can be a real boon for the shopper. Occasionally a store will even *triple* the face value of your coupons. This is rare, but it's a bonanza well worth hunting for.

I found a store a couple of miles away that fulfilled both requirements, so I adjusted my list in line with its particular sales and gave NBC the location so it could clear the filming with the manager. Needless to say, he was delighted.

And so was I when the trip worked out so much better than any of us—including myself—had expected. The look on the face of the show's producer when she heard the final total would have made the junket worthwhile—even if I hadn't saved $123.11.

Since that occasion I have taken similar shopping trips for newspapers, radio stations, and television programs from New York to San Francisco. While I guess none of them gave me quite the thrill as that initial venture, they were all a great deal of fun. I enjoyed demonstrating how shopping could be made a game rather than the drudgery most people consider it.

All these trips netted me similarly impressive savings. A trip for *The Star* in New York, for example, got me

$117.84 worth of groceries for less than $18. In Cleveland I paid $8 for purchases worth $54; that's a savings of 85 percent. In Philadelphia, taking advantage of doubling at a downtown A & P, I bought $65 worth of merchandise—and the store ended up owing me $1.67!

How much can you save with coupons?

Obviously all the trips I've described were special affairs, designed to be televised so that Supershopping could become familiar to a wider audience. It would be misleading to suggest that you will be able to realize a 95 or even 85 percent saving every time you go to the store. At the time of my NBC trip I had been cutting coupons (and bills) for over five years. I had a huge file of coupons available to choose from, and was able to use both my experience and this large stack of "winner's chips" to make an extraordinary killing at the market. On a weekly basis I can't do that, because my backlog of coupons would soon be depleted, and I'd be down to using coupons only for things that I didn't really need. And that, if you'll recall my advice in the last chapter, is something that a Supershopper never does.

On my weekly shopping trips I generally save between 40 and 60 percent of my bill. Cutting the bill in half is about normal. In other words, I'll buy $60 worth of goods, and shell out only $30. This is not as fantastic a cut as my TV trips gave me, but it sure beats paying full price.

And, you must remember, I make that 50 percent savings not just occasionally, but every time I shop. Over a year this really adds up. Last year, Steve and I estimate, we put over $1,000 in the bank as a result of couponing alone.

So, Step Two of the System is definitely "worth it."

# Why Not Cash In?

There are some interesting statistics associated with couponing that show something about both the food industry's eagerness to make it easy for us to buy (and save), and the Normal Shopper's strange reluctance to take them up on it. The statistics show, for example, that although the manufacturers are spending more and more money each year issuing coupons, the American public seems no more anxious today to cash in on the company offers than it was when the first coupon was printed eighty-four years ago. Coupons, it seems, are still a little mysterious to many of us; we use them only on a haphazard, almost incidental basis.

Actually, there's nothing at all mysterious about them. Since the C. W. Post company issued the first penny-off coupon in 1895, they have always functioned as the most visible and most widely distributed promotional scheme in the industry's whole bag of tricks. Almost everyone has used a coupon at one time or another. The Agriculture Department estimates that four out of five families are at least occasional clippers, and this is not really surprising. No matter how disorganized or opposed to "gimmicks" you may be, occasional couponing is not a great deal of trouble. All it takes is a pair of scissors. Often you don't even need to buy products to acquire them because the companies mail them to selected "occupants" throughout the country.

Last year they sent out almost 70 billion cash-offs. That's a far cry from the few thousand that Mr. Post had printed back at the turn of the century, and it's even a big jump over the amount issued at the beginning of the 1970s.

An article in the April 1978 issue of the *National Food Review* pointed out that "much of the growth in couponing has occurred since the early 1970s." (The article is "Coupon Use in Food Marketing" by Anthony Gallo and Thomas Stucker.) Whether this growth is related to rising food costs or not is a matter of speculation, but whatever the reason, the Agriculture Department figures documenting the increase are pretty impressive.

At the beginning of the decade, for example, only about 350 manufacturers were using coupons, at a total value of

$191 million. By 1976 both those figures had doubled, and the number of coupons issued was up to 46 billion. In 1977 the companies—now up to over a thousand firms—sent out 62 billion coupons, and in 1978 they upped that to 70 billion, with a new face value of $500 million!

Yet the strange thing is that, of this total, *very few were ever redeemed.* Of the 62 billion coupons issued in 1977, fewer than 3 billion were actually cashed in at supermarket registers. That left 59 billion of them lying around somewhere, eventually to end up as scrap paper, kitty litter, or confetti.

Think of the waste! If fewer than 3 billion redemptions added up to a face value of *half a billion* dollars, think how much money the manufacturers would be paying us back if we redeemed the other 59 billion. It would amount to a little under $10 billion.

Why the shoppers of America are not cashing in on this bonanza I don't know. But I do know that I'm doing my part to see to it that the redemption rate rises above the going average of less than 10 percent. If you're a Supershopper, you'll do your part as well. The manufacturers are continuing to increase the volume of coupons issued each year, begging us to try their products by offering us substantial savings if we do. I consider it my public duty to take them up on their offers.

Not only the manufacturers, but the stores themselves want you to do it. Coupons are still the firms' principal way of getting you to try new products. When a 1972 *Supermarket News* survey asked almost nine thousand shoppers what most often led them to buy a new product, almost 40 percent said "coupons." And store managers have nothing against that.

Moreover, manufacturers give stores hefty handling fees in addition to the face value of the redeemed coupons. In 1977, these fees amounted to another $150 million beyond the $500 million that the coupons themselves were worth. As a result, many individual stores are reaping their own bonanza on coupons, as the big companies allow them up to a nickel a coupon for handling.

So if you have any idea that store owners will give you baleful glances for exercising your "coupon power," forget it. Multiply that 5 cents per coupon by the nearly 3 billion turned in in 1977, and you'll see that redeeming them is no great hardship on the stores. Unless a store manager has totally forgotten where his own best interests lie, he won't resent reimbursing you for couponing—even if you do look like the Old Woman in the Shoe.

And don't feel bashful about using coupons in a store featuring doubling. The extra money the supermarket gives you beyond the face value of your coupons is absorbed by the store as advertising and promotion expenses. The store's managers must consider doubling an effective means of encouraging you to use their store or they wouldn't offer it.

There is some evidence that the redemption of coupons is on the rise, especially since the beginning of the 1970s. But it's not rising nearly fast enough to keep up with the increase in production. Between 1971 and 1977, although the *number* of coupons redeemed almost doubled, the redemption *rate* (that is, the number redeemed compared to the number issued) actually fell from 7.5 percent to under 6 percent. As we have seen that's a lot of dollars being held out and never snatched up.

To really profit from "coupon power," you have to approach couponing as a daily, enjoyable habit. That's the way you can start cutting your register tape in half every time you go to the store.

## Where to Get Coupons

You've all seen coupons before. Some people call them "cash-offs" or "cents-offs," because what they do is literally knock anywhere from 10 cents to $1 off the purchase price of the articles for which they are issued. Figure 2

Figure 2: Cents-off coupons from in-store sources, magazines, newspapers, and home mailers.

shows some of these common cents-offs. By whatever name you know them, coupons are the simplest and most easily obtainable way of cashing in at the checkout.

The first thing the novice couponer needs to know is where to get them. There are numerous ways to obtain coupons. *Here are the most common:*

## 1. In the store

Many coupons come in specially marked packages at the store. The most direct way that manufacturers choose to acquaint the shopper with new products or special offers is to enclose within their products coupons either for a second purchase of those products or for one of their other products. Many coupons are printed right on the outside of the packages. Others are inside. When a coupon is enclosed in a package, it will be so advertised on the outside. Naturally the Supershopper prefers to buy products with coupons rather than those without.

This is assuming, of course, that the price difference between the special package and the regular package is not so great as to neutralize the attraction of the coupon. If you're choosing between two national brands, a 69-cent can of artichokes with a 10-cents-off coupon inside really costs no less than a 59-cent can without the coupon—so you may as well, in such a case, take the lower-priced brand.

## 2. Magazines and newspapers

Newspapers carry not only national coupons, but what the market people call "in-ad" coupons: that is, cash-offs being offered, usually for one week only, by individual local stores. Obviously both can save you money. Checking the midweek and Sunday papers will give you an idea of where you can save the most on local coupons each week. At the same time you can clip the national coupons, which are good for a much longer time.

As for magazines, nearly every large-circulation magazine in the country features grocery and household coupons on a regular basis. The best sources are of course the
"women's magazines," which you pick up at the supermarket checkout—*Family Circle, McCall's, Ladies' Home
Journal, Woman's Day,* and so on. But coupons also appear
almost every week in *TV Guide, Reader's Digest,* and
nearly every other general interest periodical.

Subscribing to a lot of magazines, therefore, is one way
to insure yourself a steady supply of coupons. But subscription is not the only path. A more ingenious and frugal
way of getting magazine coupons is to trade them with
your friends. I have an arrangement with my neighbor Mar-
lene, for example, whereby she gives me all her dog food
coupons and I save her all my coffee ones. You can also
simply ask friends to save you those coupons they don't
use.

Doctors' and dentists' waiting rooms are another good
source. I always carry scissors with me when I bring my
children to the doctor, and I generally manage to find at
least three or four cash-offs I can use. This may seem a bit
indelicate, but not when you remember that, if some savvy
Supershopper didn't remove these coupons, they'd soon
end up in the trash, like money thrown away. And no doctor I know likes to see money thrown away.

Carole Kratz and Albert Lee, who wrote *Coupons, Rebates, Refunds,* give a couple more suggestions for acquiring magazine coupons. One is to buy old magazines in bulk
from a magazine wholesaler, such as Publishers Clearing
House, 382 Main Street, Port Washington, New York. Such
purchases can give you huge supplies of coupons at one
shot—and they will cost you only a fraction of the cover
price of the magazines. The other suggestion is to keep an
eye out for neighborhood paper drives, and offer the spon-
soring organization a small fee for letting you clip coupons
from their collections before they are bundled for resale.

You can probably come up with other ways to fill up your

coupon file from magazines. In general, just remember that almost all magazines contain some cash-offs. Keep that in mind whenever you thumb through one. (I'm not suggesting, of course, that you snip through library or bookstand copies.)

## 3. Home mailers

I don't suppose there's anyone in the country who hasn't at one time or another received a letter addressed to "Resident" or "Occupant." Manufacturers periodically send out advertising circulars to whole neighborhoods of people, and frequently these "direct mailers" or "home mailers" contain coupons.

Coupons received in the mail seem to be very popular with the American shopper. While the overall redemption rate for coupons is well under 10 percent, the rate for home mailers can go as high as 25 percent. Naturally this makes them popular with manufacturers as well, and for the past several years they have consistently increased the number of flyers-with-coupons they send out. Donnelley Marketing, distributor of the popular "Carol Wright" cents-off ensembles, increased the value of its mailers from $300 million in 1978 to a record $400 million in 1979. So, if you haven't received a home mailer lately, your turn may be coming up.

The nice thing about home mailers is that you don't have to put in any effort to obtain them. As long as you're an "occupant" (and everybody is an occupant of something), they'll eventually come to you.

You can speed up the process, however, by becoming an active refunder (see Chapter 4). As soon as I sent in for my first cash refund, I found that I had mysteriously gotten onto several manufacturers' mailing lists, and I started receiving home mailers on practically a weekly basis.

Home mailers, according to some, come under the heading of "junk mail." While I am no big fan of unsolicited advertising, I can't quite bring myself to think of coupons that save me up to a dollar on a single item as "junk."

But then Supershoppers are biased: they're in favor of saving money.

## The Simplest Way to File

Now that you have all those coupons, what are you going to do with them?

There is one quality that distinguishes the casual couponer, who is content with penny-ante saving, from the Supershopper, who goes for the highest dividends possible. That quality is a willingness to *organize*.

Now don't back away in annoyance, saying you "can't do that." Remember what I said in Chapter 2 about overcoming the tendency to consider yourself irrational. If you have ever planned a family meal, or a day's chores, or what your child is going to wear to school, then you have the organizational ability to understand and profit from my filing system.

Besides, it's the simplest system in the world. All it takes is one large envelope and a rubber band.

I know there are couponers who have developed more complicated systems for keeping track of their cash-offs. One person I knew in Ohio had a beautiful old wooden mail sorter in her kitchen, and she kept her coupons filed in the pigeonholes. Many people thumbtack their coupons to a bulletin board so they can see them easily, and others keep theirs tucked, in glorious disarray, behind cookie jars, in cookbooks, and scattered over counters. All of these methods, I guess, work all right for the people who use them. I prefer my one big envelope.

I keep the envelope in a top drawer in my kitchen cabinet. In it I place all the coupons I currently have in stock, filed alphabetically according not to brand name but to the *type* of product they're for. Your categories may be different from mine, depending on the size and nature of your family. But to give you an idea of my single-envelope system, here are the categories that I prefer to use:

| | | |
|---|---|---|
| Baby Products | Dog Food | Peanuts and |
| Batteries | Drug Items | Peanut Butter |
| Breads | Frankfurters | Pickles |
| Cakes | Frozen Foods | Pizza |
| Candy | Household | Popcorn |
| Canned Goods | Ice Cream | Rice |
| Cheese | Juices | Snacks |
| Coffee | Light Bulbs | Soda |
| Crackers and | Noodles | Spices |
| Cookies | Oil | Tea |
| | Paper Goods | |

Some of these categories contain coupons for several different kinds of items. "Drug Items," for example, includes deodorants, toothpastes, and all kinds of "notions." "Household" contains cleansers, garbage bags, mopheads, and so on. And there must be a dozen kinds of fruits and vegetables in "Canned Goods" and "Frozen Foods." Practice has taught me where to look for what I need.

Behind the "Tea" coupons I put all my rain checks—the certificates that stores give you when they are out of an advertised special, so you can buy at the advertised price when the item is back in stock. After the rain checks I alphabetically group coupons for free samples, which, like cash-offs themselves, often come in specially marked packages. All told I have about two hundred coupons in the envelope at any one time—about half of them cash-offs and half of them for free samples.

Needless to say, it's not a slender envelope. I keep it secure with a strong rubber band, and when I get new coupons (which is just about every day), I first put them under the rubber band on the outside of the envelope. Then I file them alphabetically when I have an extra five minutes or so—about every week or ten days. It's the simplest filing system imaginable, and it takes almost no time at all.

One important point to remember about coupons, though: Most cash-offs have an expiration date (ED) printed on them somewhere, and no matter how clear your filing is, if you let them sit in the envelope or drawer beyond that date, you're going to be out of luck. You'll often find that magazine and newspaper coupons are good "for 30 days" or "for 90 days." This means 30 or 90 days from the periodical's date of issue. Whenever I file new coupons, I keep an eye out for those EDs, and pull any coupons that are about to lapse, so I can try to fit them in to my next shopping trip before they do.

This is especially important at the end of the calendar year, since a great many coupons expire on December 31. Some couponers highlight the expiration dates with a yellow Magic Marker, or simply circle them. This makes them easier to see, both for you and for the checker.

## Tips for Shopping with Coupons

When I'm about to go shopping, the first thing I do, like any good Supershopper, is to check the local sales. This helps me decide which store I am going to use this week, and believe me, that varies quite a lot. While I wouldn't go very far out of my way for a few 10- or 15-cent coupons, if I'm shopping armed with a batch of valuable 50-cent and $1 cash-offs, I consider traveling a must if I can track down a nearby store that's doubling.

After deciding which store can save me the most money, I get its weekly flyer and circle the specials that interest me. Then I go to my bulging envelope and thumb through it to see which coupons I can apply to which specials, and pull them to take with me. Even though I have two hundred coupons to look at, I'm pretty familiar with my file by now, and the check never takes more than five minutes. Which is nothing, considering the savings it leads to.

Armed with the store's own "in-ad" coupons and a batch of manufacturers' cash-offs, I head for the store.

Since I've done my planning before, I meet few surprises when I get there. I may discover that oranges have shot up to 15 cents apiece, but I'll have a Minute Maid coupon with me, which will allow me to get three cans of orange juice for the price the Normal Shopper is paying for two. Or I may find that ground chuck has just jumped to the price that sirloin was last week, but I'll be able to compensate for this by using a 35-cents-off coupon on Oscar Mayer franks.

What can you use coupons for?

The answer is: practically everything. There are very few products in the modern supermarket that you can't at least occasionally discount with coupons. You can see by my list of categories in the last section that manufacturers regularly offer savings on pretty much everything, from soup to nuts. Realizing substantial savings on your food bill, then, is only a matter of being sure you have the relevant cash-offs with you when you enter the store.

Your most extensive savings are usually on household cleaning aids, health and beauty products, and all kinds of processed foods. The makers of fresh meat and produce don't offer very many cash-offs, although there are ways to cut your meat and produce bills with coupons. Some companies that don't sell meat, for example, will give you coupons for meat because they want you to use their products *with* the meat. Borden periodically offers cash-offs for ground beef so you will use their cheese for cheeseburgers. These coupons can save you as much as $1.50 on a single purchase. Ragú does the same thing with their spaghetti sauces.

Ragú also issues coupons for produce. A few weeks ago they sent me $2 worth of coupons for the purchase of fresh vegetables or mushrooms, presumably so I would remember their name as I was mixing the salad to go with the pasta.

Other coupons are issued as a kind of reward for buying

products. Recently, Johnson & Johnson gave out $3 in coupons to anyone who had bought any five of their products. The coupons were applicable against any grocery item; I used my $3 to buy enough salad greens for a week.

I mention these examples to show you that, even on nonprocessed foods, you can save money with coupons. On processed foods, the savings can be enormous. To give examples of all the cash-offs that are available for canned and frozen foods alone would take practically a book in itself. What you should know is that coupons are issued for nearly every item in the supermarket. When you shop with a handful of cash-offs, you find something to discount in every aisle, on every shelf, in the store.

But only, of course, if you are following my advice in Chapter 1 and buying brand names alone. When you're shopping with coupons, you must buy brand names—and you must also switch brands when the coupons call for it. It makes no sense to stick to a nondiscounted brand out of "loyalty" when a rival brand is offering a 50-cent savings. The Supershopper always switches brands if it saves money.

Of course, if you've planned the shopping with the store's specials in mind, you already know several of the brands you're going to buy before entering the store. Beyond that, your decisions in favor of Green Giant over Libby's, or vice versa, should be determined principally on the basis of who is offering the best coupon deal.

Another savings trick is to buy in large quantities, taking advantage of both coupons and sales. If beans are on sale at four cans for $1, I may buy ten cans and get no more for three weeks.

An even more dramatic example is the bulk purchase I made of toothpaste a while back. When Crest introduced their new 9-ounce tube of toothpaste, they advertised it at 89 cents a tube. Sensing a bargain, I decided to stock up. In my coupon envelope I found half a dozen 10-cents-off Crest coupons, and from friends I gathered four more. Then I went to the store and bought twenty tubes. Ten of them cost me 89 cents each, the other ten only 79 cents each—a total outlay of $16.80.

Sound extravagant? Not when you consider that a week later the normal 9-ounce price went into effect, and it turned out to be $1.49 a tube. If I had bought those twenty tubes one at a time, they would have cost me $29.80.

So not only was I able to forget about shopping for toothpaste for months, but I ended up saving $13 besides.

One final note. When you're going up and down the aisles, it's a good idea to separate in the cart items with coupons from those without. And be sure to tell the checkout clerk, before he or she starts ringing things up, that you're going to be using coupons. This simplifies things, and, in fact, some stores even ask you to give them your coupons before the tallying begins.

Which brings me to the most enjoyable part of the shopping trip—watching while those savings add up at the checkout.

## Cashing In

People often ask me what the checkout people think about somebody who uses as many coupons as I do.

"Don't they shudder when they see you coming?" they ask. I guess people who don't use coupons regularly must feel a little guilty about doing it at all—as if they're somehow cheating the store out of something. The heavy couponer like me (they think) must be a pain in the neck to them.

Well, I can assure you that's not the way the stores see it. Nearly every store employee I've come into contact with as an advocate of coupon power has been polite, helpful, and eager to learn more about my System. Frequently checkout people wish me continued good luck in my savings, and several of them have asked to subscribe to *Refundle Bundle*.

As I mentioned earlier in the chapter, it's really to the stores' advantage to be cooperative, and as a result most store personnel are courtesy itself. After all, they want you back as a customer. It's in their best interests to have you saisfied.

Now, some of your fellow shoppers may not feel so gracious about it, especially if they pull in behind you just as you pull out a pack of cash-offs. I remember the poor man who scooted in behind me the day we filmed the Betty Furness show. All the other lanes had four or five customers in them, and he must have figured that, even with two cartloads of goods, I was a better act to follow than the others.

Unfortunately, he hadn't counted on my encore: the presentation of $123 worth of coupons. The expression on his face as the checker started to ring them up was one of the greatest double-takes I've ever seen.

Most shoppers, however, are pretty nice about it. They may grouse a bit for having to wait longer in line, but I've found that, when I talk to them, explaining what I'm up to, they're generally even more receptive than the employees. Which makes sense, because they've got a lot to gain by learning about Supershopping.

When they see how much I save by couponing, most of them turn from annoyance to appreciation. I remember one woman in particular who was extremely skeptical as I laid a pile of coupons on the counter. She was, I guess, a typical Normal Shopper, the kind who feels that couponing is "just not worth the trouble."

"I cut those out once in a while," she said. "But I keep losing them, and they don't really save you very much anyway, do they?"

I introduced myself and assured her that, yes, coupons could save you very much indeed, if you went about it right. Then, as the checker rang up my pre-coupon tally, I told her about *Refundle Bundle,* and gave her my address to write to if she wanted to learn more about the System.

The total was something like $40. I saw my new friend

glance at the register, then grin as I handed over the coupons. We chatted a bit more as the coupon total rose. As the final total came up, I could see her eyebrows go up in expectation. When the checker announced, "23.90," there was another one of those double-takes that make Supershopping so much fun. The woman looked confused, then brightened and took out a pencil and paper.

"What was that address again?" she asked.

## STEP TWO: Using Coupon Power

Here are the major points to keep in mind when following Step Two of Supershopping—using coupons:

1. Clipping cents-off coupons can save you 50 percent on your grocery bill every week, but only if you use them wisely and regularly. Letting them lie in a drawer until they expire won't save you a penny.

2. Only the big national companies can afford to issue coupons. Therefore, coupon power means buying the national brand names almost exclusively.

3. You can find cents-off coupons on specially marked packages, in newspapers and magazines, and in home mailers. Trading with friends will increase your supply.

4. To profit from coupons, you have to be able to find them easily. A simple filing method is to keep your coupons arranged alphabetically under general categories in a single large envelope. Note the coupon expiration dates, so you won't get stuck with expired offers.

5. Periodically, stores in stiff competition offer double value for coupons as a means of inducing you to buy. It's definitely worthwhile hunting around for a store that's "doubling," even if it's not your "favorite" store. Doubling can mean significant extra savings.

6. Contrary to popular opinion, most store personnel are *not* offended by the heavy coupon user. Heavy couponing means good sales for the store, plus healthy handling fees. So you need not be embarrassed about using your coupon power: it benefits the store as well as the shopper.

# 4/Money in the Mail

Last winter, when our back door thermometer looked as if it were stuck at 20 below, Steve and I bundled ourselves up, packed our suitcases full of swimsuits, shorts, and tee shirts, and took a plane to Florida. For two glorious weeks, while our New York neighbors were cursing their snow shovels, we soaked up the sun and told ourselves that we'd have to do this every year.

We are not wealthy. Up until a few years ago, we were both schoolteachers, and even our combined salary was barely enough to cover expenses in the midst of the mid-seventies' recession. When we bought a house in 1973, we soon started thinking that we must have been crazy: the mortgage payments were so bad that we once considered telling the bank, "Take the house, we give up."

For years, saving money looked like some fairy-tale dream: something that, no matter how hard we tried, would always remain just beyond our grasp.

How was it, then, that we were able last year to winter under the palms?

The answer is Step Three of my Supershopping System: a tax-free savings plan called refunding.

While coupon clipping has enabled me to cut our shopping bill in half for the past several years, refunding has given us a secure and steady fund of emergency money that has made it possible for us to realize some of our "impossible" dreams—such as a January without icicles.

## How You Benefit by Refunding

Like couponing, refunding is a promotional scheme devised by the food manufacturers to get shoppers to try, and keep on buying, their products. Like coupons, refunds (or "rebates," as some refunders call them) are a simple and certain way of saving money at the supermarket. Like couponing, effective refunding relies on daily clipping, using national brands exclusively, and occasionally buying in bulk.

There are, however, major differences between Step Two and Step Three of the System.

First, while coupons are redeemed in the store at the time you buy the product, your refund will come to you in the form of a check, usually some weeks after you've sent in for it.

Second, you can realize savings with coupons merely by presenting them, and them alone, at the time of purchase, while many refund offers require you to mail in not only a *proof of purchase* but also an entry blank called a *refund form* (or *required blank*) as well, before you can receive your check.

Finally, the face value of most coupons is between 10 and 50 cents; it's a rare cash-off that discounts you over $1 (unless you're doubling). Refunds, on the other hand, generally *start* around 25 or 50 cents, and can run as high as $4 or $5. This means that, although refunding takes a little more time than coupon clipping, the extra savings make it well worth it.

_Here's how refunding works:_

**1.** The manufacturer issues an offer of a refund to all customers who have bought a particular product of that company. Lipton, for example, recently offered a refund of $1.50 on their dried soup mixes, and advertised it in stores with pads of the necessary forms attached to the shelves next to the products.

**2.** You, the shopper, take one of the refund forms, fill it out, and mail it in to the address given, accompanied by whatever proofs of purchase are required. Lipton, in this case, asked for the front-name panels from any five cartons of their soups.

**3.** The form, with your proof of purchase, reaches its destination, which is generally not the manufacturer but an organization known as a _redemption agency_ or _clearinghouse_, which processes the refund in the manufacturer's name. The address on the Lipton form, for example, was a post office box in Clinton, Iowa—and Clinton is the home of the nation's largest clearinghouse, the A. C. Nielsen Company. Nielsen processes not only refund forms sent from individuals, but also redeemed coupons sent from retail stores. This means that, if you are an active couponer and refunder, a lot of your mail is ending up in Iowa.

**4.** The clearinghouse checks that you have sent the proper labels, panels, or other proofs to qualify for the offer—proofs of purchase, in fact, are often referred to as "qualifiers." Then it mails you a check in the manufacturer's name.

This whole process usually takes about four to eight weeks, from the time you mail off your qualifiers to the time the post office delivers your check. The Lipton form asks you to "please allow six weeks for delivery," and this, in my experience, is a fair estimate of a refunder's waiting time.

That's it in a nutshell. You buy a product. You save the carton. You send it in to the company's representative. And they pay you for having bought it.

## Realizing the Biggest Dividends

That is how refunding works on its own, and it can be extremely profitable even if used just by itself, but you'll realize the greatest savings if you use it in conjunction with couponing, as described in the previous chapter. The beauty of Supershopping as a system is that all its steps lock together to form a profitable whole. The expert couponer is the most likely candidate to earn big dividends as a refunder, and vice versa.

Consider, for example, my bulk purchase of Crest, which I discussed in the last chapter. I bought those twenty tubes, as I explained, principally because I knew that I'd save money right away by doing so—by buying them at an introductory markdown. In addition, I used coupons to further reduce their price. But even beyond that, I stocked up on that much toothpaste because, as a long-time refunder, I knew that at some time in the near future Crest would be offering $1 or $2 back for the presentation of a given number of their toothpaste cartons. I actually ended up saving three ways: by the original discount, by the couponing cash-off, and by a future refund. This is what refunders call the Triple Play.

Regular refunding, combined with couponing, can sometimes make you feel a little embarrassed at how well you're doing. When you refund as often as I do, you soon find yourself on numerous mailing lists, and are constantly opening envelopes full of cash-offs, two-for-one coupons, certificates for free samples—all of this in addition to the regular, daily refund checks.

There are certain products, as a result, that I haven't laid out money for in two or three years—among them, spaghetti sauce, toilet tissue, paper towels, and various kinds of candy.

In Chapter 6 I'll talk more about how using the steps of my System together can assure you a steady supply of free samples and gifts. Now I just want to stress that refunding, when it's used with the steps I've discussed already, can be the knockout punch of a super savings combination.

Money, of course, is the bottom line. It's hard to describe the pleasure a new refunder feels when she opens the mailbox and discovers that first refund check. (See Figure 3 for an illustration of sample refund checks.) I got my first one—a $1 rebate for buying Del Monte canned goods—about six years ago, and I can still recall the delight of feeling that I was on to something important. How important, I didn't even imagine. Certainly I never thought, as I admired that "thanks for buying" money from Del Monte, that within a few years I would be receiving enough similar checks to finance a Florida vacation!

In the last chapter I mentioned how strange it was that so few coupons are redeemed, out of the billions issued. What is even stranger is how few shoppers are wise to the advantages of refunding. Even though their redemption rate is low, 80 percent of American shoppers still do use coupons on at least a casual basis. You would think that a system that guarantees you'll receive checks almost daily in the mail would gain at least as many converts. But for some reason that isn't so. According to Department of Agriculture estimates, the number of shoppers who refund regularly is only about one in four!

Everybody has heard of coupons, but when I talk to other shoppers about refund offers, I very seldom sense more than a dim appreciation of what I'm talking about. Yet the system, as you've seen, is not complicated at all. Why do so few people use it?

The major reason, I suspect, is simply that most people

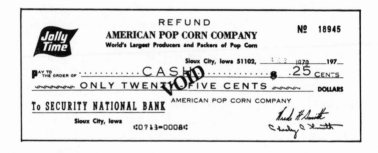

Figure 3: Your refund checks will look something like these.

still don't know about it. Coupons are hard to miss. They wave at us from every magazine, every newspaper, every specially marked package in the land. Refunds, on the other hand, are fairly obscure. Many shoppers don't even recognize a refund form when they see one. And many forms, sad to say, disappear from the stores before their time because of theft.

But there are other reasons for their lack of popularity. Some shoppers are under the mistaken notion that cashing in with refunds involves buying truckloads of items you don't want. Others, without ever trying the system, presume that anything that guarantees you a steady extra income must be either a lot of trouble or illegal.

Neither of these suppositions is correct. What I want to do in the remainder of this chapter is to outline my refunding system in some detail, clearing up the misconceptions and explaining how refunding brings me approximately $1,500 *each year* in tax-free extra income.

How can refund money be tax-free? The IRS looks at money sent to you for having bought certain brands not as income, but as a reduction in the purchase price of the articles purchased. They make no distinction here between coupons and refund checks, to our great advantage.

## Three Easy Steps: The Refunder's S.O.S.

If you're like I was before I developed my System, you sometimes feel financially as if you're on a desert island with very little food or water. Well, couponing can be a way of making the available supplies stretch, but refunding can be the means that finally gets you rescued. To make it work properly, however, you have to follow what I call "the Refunder's S.O.S."

Just as the dedicated couponer can realize savings far in excess of those realized by the casual clipper, so, too, the dedicated refunder can profit enormously if he or she approaches refunding not so much as a hobby (although it is a fascinating one) as a matter of immediate financial need. I know it was the combination of coupons and refunding that bailed us out of our financial bind. But that was only because I had gradually learned how to send up an appropriate call of distress.

When you're stranded on a desert island, you can't just thrash your arms about and scream wildly, hoping someone will hear you. You've got to go about getting rescued in as cool and organized a manner as possible, or you'll simply end up getting hoarse.

First, like Robinson Crusoe, you've got to believe you will survive. Then *(at the risk of straining my metaphor to the breaking point)* you must do three things:

1. **Save** everything you can find that might help you.

2. **Organize** your time and labor as efficiently as possible, to make the best use of what you find.

3. **Send** out messages for help—bottles, smoke signals, bonfires—on a regular, consistent basis.

## Save Everything: It's Valuable

In the last section I mentioned *proofs of purchase* and said that, in order to get cash refunds, you have to send them in along with the relevant entry forms. Actually, when refunders talk about proofs of purchase, they mean two things.

One definition of proof of purchase, or POP, is a sticker or section of a package that actually contains the phrase "proof of purchase," or something similar, such as "purchase confirmation" or "purchase seal." Such a seal—generally enclosed within a dotted line—is put on packages specifically to serve as your proof of having bought the product. (See Figure 4 for sample POP seals.)

Figure 4: Proof of purchase seals, like these, are easy to spot.

Figure 5: UPC seals stand out like keys on a piano—but they are all different.

But there is another, broader definition of proof of purchase. Manufacturers frequently change the part of their packaging that they will accept as proof of purchase, and you may find that such other parts of a box as the net weight statement, the box top (or bottom), the ingredient panel, the tear strip, or the Universal Product Code (UPC) seal are requested in refund offers in lieu of the actual POP seal. (Figure 5 illustrates typical UPC seals.) In these cases, whatever part of the packaging is requested is really being used as a proof of purchase. To avoid confusion between the specific and the general use of the term, refunders usually refer to any packaging part being requested as a _qualifier_, and reserve the use of the term "proof of purchase" for the actual POP seals.

The point to remember here, though, is that you can never tell when you buy a product which part of its packaging will eventually be required as a qualifier. Pampers, which for years required the size designation oval as proof, recently changed to asking for the words "Disposable Diapers," for example.

The moral is that, if you want to really profit from refunding, you must save _everything_.

According to Carole Kratz and Albert Lee, authors of _Coupons, Refunds, Rebates_, "The average American family discards about $3.00 worth of labels _every day_." Since you don't know what part of a box will later qualify you for a dollar back, you simply have to keep the whole thing, and cut off the relevant portions when the time comes.

The same rule should apply to bottles: save not only the front labels but also the neck labels and the cap liners or inner seals. With canned goods, save the entire label. (Figures 6 and 7 are diagrams of a "typical" box and bottle, with arrows identifying which parts of the packaging might someday be asked for as qualifiers.)

In addition, the wise refunder also saves her cash register receipts. Because some dishonest shoppers occasionally remove proofs of purchase in the store without buying the

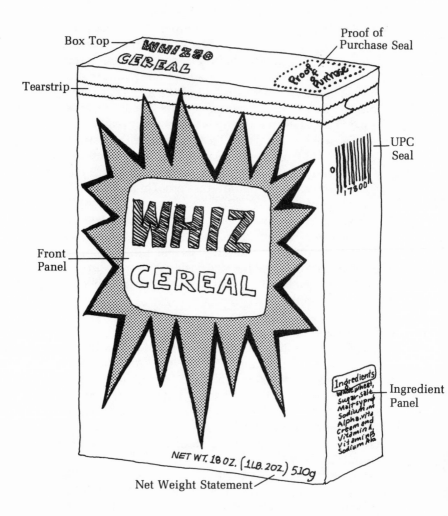

Figure 6: A typical box has many elements that might be worth money to you.

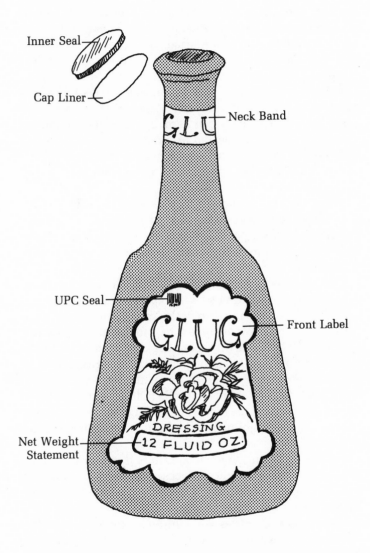

Figure 7: Many of the packaging elements of a bottle are useful to supershoppers.

product, the companies from time to time may ask you to furnish them with the original or a copy of your sales slip, with the relevant purchase price circled, as an extra proof that you have in fact bought the product and not just clipped out the POP.

This doesn't happen very often, but it pays to be safe rather than sorry. Unfortunately, the level of "misredemption," such as that described here, is not decreasing, so the companies may be expected to increase their cash receipt spot checks. Practice will teach you whether or not it's worth it to you to go to the small extra trouble of saving such receipts.

Naturally, saving everything means that at any one time you are likely to have on hand a goodly supply of packaging and packaging parts. But you need not feel as if you're living in a paper recycling plant if you follow a few simple guidelines.

First, you should try to make your qualifiers as small as possible. The method I use with boxes (such as cereal and detergent boxes) is to remove the inner wrapper (companies seldom ask for that since it has no identifying marks), then peel off the thick cardboard backing until I'm left with the outer covering alone: the part with the writing on it. A sharp knife or razor is helpful here, although your fingernails will do just about as well. (Other refunders have found that wetting the boxes and letting them sit in a large plastic bag overnight makes the front covering even easier to peel off.)

Finally, I flatten the emaciated box down until it's the thickness of just a couple of pieces of typing paper, and put a rubber band around groups of them to secure them. This makes them a lot easier to store.

With cans and bottles you simply steam or soak off the labels in hot water. You can throw out the bottle caps (keeping the liners) and bottles themselves, since redemption for such heavy items long ago proved too much trouble for the manufacturers.

Peeling off cardboard backings and soaking off labels may not be your idea of a high old time, but it's surprising how quickly you can get to like the chore when you know there's money in it for you.

Many refunders even manage to have fun doing it. One refunder in Colorado, whom I met through _Refundle Bundle_, has made a regular Saturday morning ritual of label soaking and box slicing—with the whole family involved. She and her husband peel off cardboard backings while their two children, aged eight and ten, slosh the empty bottles around in the sink. To them it's a game, but at the end of an hour or so of soaking in warm soapy water, the labels come off easily. Then the kids stick them up against the inside of the kitchen cabinets, where they stay until they are dry and ready for storage. (Refunder Victor Grillio of Walden, New York, warns that the "stick-up" method works best on smooth surfaces such as Contac paper, tile, Formica, or window glass. The labels tend to mar surfaces of wood or paint.)

Which brings me to the O part of my refunding S.O.S.—organizing the qualifiers into a compact and workable storage space, where they can stay until they're ready to make you money.

## Secrets for Easy Organizing

Now that you have all those qualifiers, where on earth will you put them?

The most common complaint I hear from new refunders is that their living space is being gobbled up by packaging. "It's like I'm living in a blizzard of qualifiers," one woman said to me. "I have so many of the things I can't put my finger on the one I want when I want it."

I asked this woman what kind of filing system she uses, and she stared at me as if she were puzzled.

"Why, I don't have any special system, I guess. Some are

on my counter, some are in canisters, and . . . well, I just never thought about filing them."

"Think about it," I advised. And I explained to her the importance of organization.

At any one time I probably have up to a thousand different qualifiers in my house, ready to be tapped when needed. My memory is pretty good, but I'm certainly not so foolhardy as to rely on it alone to keep track of that many box tops, seals, and labels. Over the years experience has taught me that the refunder who makes the most money is the one who can find any required qualifier as soon as it's needed, without having to turn the house upside down in the process. This means that, if you're going to negotiate Step Three successfully, you need a workable filing system.

It need not be elaborate. Very few refunders, I would guess, are certified public accountants on the side; few of us can afford to be bothered with shelves of ledgers, in- and out-baskets, and other paraphernalia. But we do all share a simple recognition: the sooner you can dig up your proofs, the sooner you'll get that check.

My filing system is, I think, fairly typical of other refunders' systems. All it takes is a plastic produce bag, a few shoe boxes, and one large envelope.

The plastic bag I keep in a drawer, and whenever I get a bunch of qualifiers, I toss them in until I'm ready to file them. Generally it takes three or four weeks until the bag is full, and at that point I haul it out and go to my shoe boxes.

I have six of these, half of them boot size, plus one large box (24″ × 18″ × 10″). All are kept out of the way in the garage. In them I file my flattened-down qualifiers, arranged alphabetically according to product name. The smaller labels and cartons go into the shoe size, the larger ones into the boot size. The whole thing takes up about a 2′ × 2′ space—which makes it compact as well as efficient.

To give you an idea of what my file for smaller items looks like, here are the product names of the qualifiers I keep in the shoe boxes:

Aunt Millie's
Borden
Buitoni
Bumble Bee
Campbell's
Carnation
Chef Boy·Ar·Dee
Chicken of the Sea
Chun King
College Inn
Cycle Dog Food
Del Monte
Dole
Gerber
Hawaiian Punch
Heinz
Hellman's
Hi-C
Jif
Ken-L Ration
Kleenex
Kraft
La Choy
Lawry's
Libby's

Lipton
Log Cabin
Mazola
Milkbone
Mott's
Ocean Spray
Ovaltine
Peter Pan
Planters
Pledge
Progresso
Ragú
Ronzoni
Sanka
Smucker's
Skippy
Star Kist
Stokely
Sun Giant Almonds
Sunsweet
Tang
Uncle Ben's
Van Camp
V-8
Welch's
Wesson Oil

Your list will vary according to what you buy.

In addition to these shoe boxes, I have three boot boxes in which I keep qualifiers arranged according to types of products, since for certain items this seems an easier method for me. In the first boot box I have margarine boxes, cream cheese boxes and wrappers, and cocoa and noodle boxes. I know that may seem an eccentric combination, but it works for me. In the second boot box I file qualifiers from toothpaste, pizza, batteries, drugs, and plastic bags such as Glad and Hefty. In the third one I keep qualifiers from frozen food, coffee, cereals, crackers, candy, frozen cakes, cookies, and disposable cups.

Finally, I have one large box, about two feet long and a foot and a half deep. It holds salad dressing labels, soap wrappers, detergent boxes, tea boxes, paper towel wrappers, and labels from plastic bottles, such as Final Touch and Joy.

That's the entire system. Six boxes, arranged with a combination of alphabetical regularity and (I admit) personal caprice. But I'm so thoroughly familiar with what I have that I never have to hunt for what I want.

Most refunders use systems similar to this one. Some file their qualifiers in larger cartons, and some prefer to keep all proofs for, say, Bold detergent in an empty but unflattened box of Bold itself. But most of us agree that, considering the bulkiness of qualifiers, filing in boxes is easier than filing in metal or wooden cabinets. (It's cheaper, too.)

Many new refunders worry that a file such as this will take up so much space that their families will have to sleep on the roof. They needn't worry. As I mentioned, my entire shoe-box operation takes up only about 4 square feet of floor space, and some refunders, who are more strapped for space than we are, make even more efficient use of small areas.

Many refunders, it's curious to note, live or have lived in mobile homes, and have therefore had to learn how to squeeze the last drop of juice *into* the orange, so to speak. A Florida refunder we met last winter keeps nearly thirty cartons of qualifiers on a roll-out platform under her bed. You'd be surprised what a little energetic stacking and squeezing can accomplish.

So much for the qualifier file. The other thing you will want to keep track of is your refund forms. These I keep, as

I keep my cash-offs, in a single large business envelope, filed alphabetically by product and with the expiration date circled. Since there are only about one hundred of these at any one time, and since I check them frequently, it's never a problem finding the ones I want.

Some refunders prefer to use a small filing box for forms, and some like to file them chronologically according to expiration date. Either of these techniques is fine, and you should use whatever system works for you. You'll know it's working if you can pull the appropriate forms and qualifiers without upending the house—and if you can do so, consistently, without finding that three-quarters of them have expired.

One way I avoid this is to pull selected forms as their expiration dates approach, and paper clip them onto whatever qualifiers I have toward the offer. I keep these packets nearing expiration dates in a top kitchen drawer, and as I acquire new proofs, I simply add them to the packets rather than filing them in my shoe boxes. This way I keep down to the bare minimum the number of "passed ED" disappointments.

There is one more aspect to refunding organization that you may want to consider, and that is keeping a running record of what refunds you have sent away for, and when. Many refunders keep such a log to be able to check up on the companies periodically and see whether there are any outstanding refunds that they might reasonably expect in short order. They arrange their logs in column order in a notebook, with headings for the company name and address, what qualifiers were sent and when, and the name and amount of the refund. As the checks come in, they mark them off in a final, "Received" column.

There's nothing wrong with keeping this kind of record, and if you have the time and inclination I'd say go right ahead. Certainly it provides you with a quick and accurate way of determining who owes you what—and of seeing, over time, how much money you've made on refunding. It also teaches you which companies are the most prompt and reliable in sending refunds.

But personally I don't find record keeping necessary. The companies have always been quite honest with me, and since only a small fraction of refund requests go astray in the mail, I don't feel it's worth my time to check up on all of them. I suppose I must lose track of some offers this way, but probably not enough to make much of a dent in that yearly $1,500. When I send in for a refund, I like to forget about it until it arrives—at which time it's like a pleasant, almost unexpected surprise.

But to be "surprised" like this on a daily basis, you have to practice, without fail, the final part of my Refunder's S.O.S. You must send in for those checks.

## How to Receive Checks Regularly

Sending for your money on a regular, consistent basis is very important. No matter how well managed your filing is, it will do you no good unless you make it a point to ask for your checks as often as an offer becomes available and you have the necessary qualifiers. The companies are now sending me an average of about $125 a month in refund checks, but that is only because I am religious about writing them. I send out about one hundred letters a month, just to keep up that $125 monthly average return.

"Doesn't that take a lot of time?" I'm often asked.

In fact, it doesn't. The *total* amount of time I spend on refunding—this includes clipping, filing forms, arranging qualifiers, *and* sending for the offers—never exceeds five or six hours a week. That's less than an hour a day.

There are plenty of ways to cut down on refunding time. It's easy to cut corners on the actual sending part of the process. I do most of my filling in of forms and addressing of envelopes, for example, while I'm also doing something else: riding in the car, watching television, or just waiting for the water to boil. When I play Mah-Jongg, I address madly when it's my turn to be out, and before long, addressing ceases to be a chore and becomes, like knitting, a diverting conversational aid.

The principal thing to remember about the time spent on refunding is that, if you start to see it as drudgery, you'll soon defeat the purpose of the game. After all, it ought to be fun to save. If you arrange your time so that addressing envelopes is something you do along with something else, before you know it you'll have fifty forms in the mail, and be on your way to becoming $50 richer next month.

*Beyond that, there are a couple of points to keep in mind as you write the companies.*

1. Be sure that whatever qualifiers you're sending are precisely the ones they've requested. If an offer calls for the net weight seals from two small-size boxes of Duz, it generally will not honor the seal from one (or even two) large-size boxes. A refunder friend from North Carolina was recently refused a refund because she sent the Ralston Purina Company a label from a puppy food when their offer had specified "adult dog food." There are occasional exceptions, but in general you must give them exactly what they ask for, or you'll be out of luck.

2. Before you send the form in, check to see that it has not expired. This will avoid your receiving one of those embarrassing letters that begin "We regret to inform you ..." Once in a while a company, to keep you in its good graces, will extend an offer beyond the date printed on the form; they do this especially if the closing date is near when you write them for a form, and they realize you can't possibly get it in on time. But extension is not something you can count on, so you should be careful about keeping an eye on those EDs before the date gets too close.

3. Be patient. Many novice refunders have complained to me that their refunds "just aren't coming." Hold on a while, and they will. The clearinghouses have to pro-

cess a large volume of forms, and as a result, getting your money can sometimes take even more time than the forms themselves indicate it will. Don't give up. The companies are, almost without exception, quite honorable in their dealings with refunders, and unless you have waited in vain for, say, three or four months, I'd advise you not to write them a letter of complaint.

If you simply can't wait any longer, a brief, polite note stating the name of the refund and the date you sent it in will get you your check a lot faster than an attack on their policies or integrity. Send it to the Customer Services Department of the company that offered the refund.

That's my Refunder's S.O.S. You should always remember that the more work you put into this rewarding hobby, the less it will seem like a hobby and the more it will take on the attributes of a home-based moneymaking venture. Which, of course, is exactly what it is.

At the same time, you should not be putting so much work into it that it ceases to give you pleasure. I suppose that if I put in ten or twelve hours a week on refunding, I might be getting back several hundred dollars more a year than I am, and if you feel up to that kind of investment of time, it may prove worth your while. For me, an hour a day for $1,500 a year seems just about right.

## Where to Find Those All-Important Forms

Not all refund offers require forms. For many of the cashback offers you'll read about, all you have to do is send in the qualifiers with your name and address and the name of the offer, such as "One dollar refund on Cap'n Crunch, in exchange for five box tops." In addition, some offers that do require forms are honored even without them. But, like the extension of expiration dates, this is not something you can absolutely count on.

The offers that do ask for forms (or "required blanks") are highly prized by refunders, largely because a heavy percentage of the really big rebates—the $2 to $5 offers— fall into this category. So, if you're paging through a magazine and see a refund offer, check immediately to see if the form contains a phrase such as "with this coupon" or "this certificate required." It means that your request will not be honored without the form.

Where do you find them? Basically, forms are available in all the places that coupons are available, plus a couple more. *The following are the principal sources:*

1. **The stores** themselves. There are two kinds of forms you can generally pick up in the supermarket. One type, called the *store form* (SF is the refunders' common code) is found attached to shelves in tear-off pads. (Figure 8 shows typical store forms.) The customer is expected to take one of the forms, to comply with the common one-per-family rule, but some shoppers are in the habit of grabbing whole packs of them, in order to sell them to others. Deplorable as this practice is, it's unfortunately quite common, and as a result store forms are often very hard to come by. You need not despair, however, if the forms are all gone, for the pads of forms are generally attached to a cardboard backing on which the manufacturer will have printed an address to which you can write to get satisfaction.

There are two kinds of cardboard backings. (See Figure 9.) One will ask you simply to send your name and address, with the relevant qualifiers, to the given address to receive your refund. The refund shown first in Figure 9 is an example of one of these cardboard backings.

The other kind of cardboard backing (refunders call them CBs) is represented in the illustration by the second offer. This kind asks that you send your name and address to the given address to receive the required *form* rather

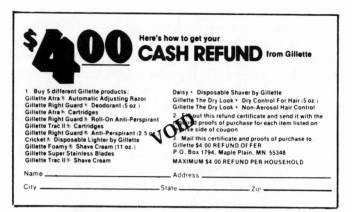

Figure 8: These are typical store forms you can find in your supermarket, usually on tear-off pads.

# FREE!

**CRICKET**

ACCENT TABLE LIGHTER

Mail-back Offer Details

Mail to:  Cricket ' Accent Lighter
P.O. Box 196 • St. Paul, Minn. 55197

I have enclosed 2 Cricket® proofs of purchase plus 50¢ for postage and handling.
Send my Accent Table Lighter to:

Name _____
Please Print

Address _____

City _____ State _____ Zip _____

# $3.00 CASH REFUND OFFER (by mail)

When you buy 4 of these 8 Alberto-Culver products!
(See details on back.)

**"Everything's Coming Up Cash" Refund**

Buy two or more of the following fine products to get a cash refund of up to $2.00:

Kleenex* Tissues 280 Sheet Family Size
Teri* Towels
New Freedom* Mini or Maxi Pads

# SORRY

All Official Refund Request Forms have been taken. You may still obtain your form by writing to:

**"Everything's Coming Up Cash" Offer**
**Post Office Box 9386**
**St. Paul, Minnesota 55193**

An Official Refund Request Form must accompany your product code symbols and a properly marked cash register receipt. Offer Expires September 30, 1979

---

## SORRY, LAST COUPON TAKEN

To obtain your $1.00 cash refund, send one empty bag of TEASER POPS™ Candy to:

Teaser Pops $1.00 Refund
P.O. Box BK
Chicago, Ill. 60677

Offer expires Dec. 31, 1979. Limit one refund per household. Offer void where prohibited, taxed or otherwise restricted. Allow 4-6 weeks for delivery.

---

## $3.00 REFUND on LIVELY LEGS®
## Maternity Panty Hose

Sorry, all coupons are gone. You can still participate in this offer by following these instructions:

Send both end panels from a pair of LIVELY LEGS Maternity Panty Hose. Include your name and address along with cash register receipt and mail to: **BAUER & BLACK Hosiery Offer**
**P. O. Box NB-439**
**El Paso, Texas 79977**

Void where prohibited, taxed, or restricted by law. Offer limited to one refund per family. **Offer expires June 30, 1979.**

Figure 9: The cardboard backing of store form pads usually contains information like this.

than the refund. To get the refund, you must then fill in the form and send it along with the appropriate qualifiers.

Cardboard backings are very important for refunders. For that reason you should avoid removing them from the shelves. Just jot down the relevant information, and you'll get your money in due order.

Another type of in-store form is the kind that appears on the products themselves. These may be actually printed on the packaging, or they may be attached to it in the form of stickers or (in the case of bottles) _hang tags_. (See Figure 10.) Sadly, hang tags (HT) have a way of disappearing rapidly, too. Stealing them is, of course, illegal.

2. **Newspapers and magazines.** These often contain forms good not only for cash refunds, but for free samples of the product, or rather for coupons worth free samples at your store. (See Figure 11.) Everything I said in the last chapter about magazine and newspaper coupons applies as well to the refund forms in such periodicals. Check the Sunday supplements especially.

3. **Home mailers.** Again, what I said in Chapter 3 about coupons also applies here, with one addition: by becoming an active refunder, you will almost certainly increase your chances of receiving forms (and coupons) through the mail. The quickest way I know to get on a refund mailing list is to send in for that first refund.

4. **The companies** themselves. Let's say your local supermarket has been the victim of one of those form hoarders I mentioned earlier, and that someone else has used the cardboard backing to obtain a store form. (This, as I've said, is not advisable.) You've heard from a friend that Loving Care Lotion is giving back $1 for two front panels, and you have the panels, but no form. What do you do?

You can write to the company directly, requesting a form. The address can be found on any box of Loving Care; remember to bring your letter to the attention of the Customer Service Department. All the major firms have such departments now, and they are usually extremely helpful

Figure 10: Hang tags are normally used on bottles.

# 50¢ Refund Offer

Campbell Soup Company will send you 50¢ in return for any 4 labels from the following "No Salt Added" Soups: Tomato Bisque, Chicken 'n Dumplings, Turkey Vegetable and Vegetable & Beef Stockpot.

Just mail the labels with your name, address and zip code to: **No Salt Added, P.O. Box 2115, Maple Plain, MN 55348**

Name_____
(Please print)

Address_____

City_____State_____Zip_____

Only requests submitted on this form will be accepted.

Offer expires June 30, 1979. Limit one refund per family, group or organization. Please allow 8 weeks for handling. Offer good only to residents of Florida. Void if taxed, restricted or forbidden by law.

TAKE ONE

SEE DETAILS ON REVERSE SIDE

75¢ MAIL REBATE

With proof-of-purchase from Dow Bathroom Cleaner and K mart® Blue Tint Toilet Bowl Cleaner

CASH IN

GET $1.00 CASH REFUND

FOR 3 NET WEIGHT STATEMENTS FROM SPECIFIED PACKAGES OF FRITO LAYS BRAND POTATO CHIPS

DETAILS ON BACK

Figure 11: Newspaper and magazine forms are very familiar to supershoppers.

to the "formless" refunder. Among the companies that are best about supplying forms are the following:

| | |
|---|---|
| American Can | Mrs. Smith's Pies |
| Axion | Pepperidge Farm |
| Breck (shampoos) | Procter & Gamble |
| Buitoni | Sara Lee Kitchens |
| Cambell's (soups) | Skippy Peanut Butter |
| Hunt-Wesson Foods | Uncle Ben's Rice |
| Johnson & Johnson | Union Carbide Company |
| La Choy | |
| Lever Bros. | Vick Chemical Company |
| Libby's | |
| Mobil Chemical Company | Welch Food |

This is a partial list, of course, and could change. (For this list I am partially indebted to the *Liberty Refunder's Yearbook,* ©1978 by Kathleen Mero of Concord, California.) In my experience, almost every company I've ever dealt with has been helpful in supplying forms.

5. **Trading.** If all else fails, you as a refunder have recourse to the single most interesting and satisfying method of obtaining forms that I know: trading, or swapping, them with your fellow refunders.

I have mentioned my newsletter *Refundle Bundle* in passing a few times, but I haven't really given you an idea of what a refunding newsletter is or how it can help you become a more successful refunder. In the following chapter I'll go into this in some detail. Here I should simply point out that subscribing to a refunding newsletter is without a doubt the single best way to receive both information about current offers, and the forms necessary to send in for them.

The main advantage of belonging to the refunding network that operates through these monthly bulletins is that it multiplies by many times the chances that you will spot, and thus be able to profit from, an available offer. Even if you searched the magazines and newspapers hours each day, you could not guarantee that you would catch every company offer by yourself. Some of them, indeed, are geared to specific local audiences, and these you would be sure to miss.

When you get a monthly bulletin, on the other hand, you automatically enlist refunders from New York to California to search along with you, and this immediately increases your chances of catching the most lucrative offers.

But a newsletter such as *Refundle Bundle* doesn't only give you the advantage of thousands of eyes scanning the papers for you. It also puts you in contact with many people who may have forms that you lack, and these are people who are looking to trade them with you for the forms you have that *they* lack.

By joining together, everybody profits.

## STEP THREE: Getting Paid for Shopping

Here are the most important points to remember about the central part of the Supershopping System: refunding.

1. Refunding, in which manufacturers reimburse you for buying, is the heart of the Supershopping System. It can provide you with a substantial extra savings account, tax-free.

2. You can find refund offers on specially marked packages, on store shelves, at supermarket courtesy booths, in newspapers and magazines, and in home mailers. Offers are also listed regularly in refunding newsletters.

3. Many refund offers require only that you send in your name and address with the requested "proofs of purchase" or "qualifiers." Others ask

that you send in the refund offer form as well. Form-required offers are generally a little more profitable than no-form offers.

4. Almost any part of a package may be requested as a proof of purchase. Common qualifiers include POP seals, UPC seals, box tops and bottoms, ingredients panels, front panels, neck bands, cap liners, inner seals, and tear strips. The moral is to save everything.

5. The wise refunder never buys an unneeded product just to collect needed qualifiers. You may want to buy in bulk sometimes to get necessary proofs more quickly, but you should never stock up on things you're not going to use: this would defeat the whole purpose of the System, which is to save money.

6. Remember "the Refunder's S.O.S." *Save* everything. *Organize* your qualifier file so you can find what you need when you need it. *Send* regularly for your checks.

7. When you send in for offers, be sure that you include exactly what the offer asks for, and that it has not yet expired. Then, be patient: offers sometimes take a couple of months to be processed. If you send in regularly, however, you'll regularly receive money in the mail.

# 5/ We're All in This Together

Roughly twenty-five years ago, Niles Eggleston of Milford, New York, began collecting information on refund offers and putting it together into a small, mimeographed newsletter that he named, optimistically, *Quick Silver*. That was the first refunders' newsletter.

Since August 1954, when the first issue of *Quick Silver* was sent out, to the present day, the refunding newsletter network has grown with remarkable regularity. Throughout the 1960s, when consumerism and do-it-yourself became important aspects of many alternative living styles, newsletters were founded at the rate of several each year, and that growth rate has continued even into the more sedate 1970s. Today, there are over fifty refund newsletters—or "bulletins," as they are often called—serving refunders nationwide, with more being founded every year.

Moreover, many of these small, home-based operations have begun to enjoy astonishing increases in circulation. My own *Refundle Bundle* typifies the widening interest in refunding. I started in 1973 with only thirteen subscribers, most of them neighborhood friends; today, I send the newsletter to thirty thousand monthly subscribers, spread all the way from Maine to Florida, and out to the West Coast.

This explosion of interest in newsletters is easily explained. As food prices soar, shoppers become eager to learn more about the bill-cutting system that has worked for thousands of people and so they subscribe to refunding newsletters. The central reason for the growth of the refunding "underground" is very simple: *newsletter subscribers save money*—much more of it, generally speaking, than nonsubscribers.

## How Newsletters Work for You

Refunding newsletters are privately printed, usually once a month. These guides list current cash rebate offers and information for swapping forms and/or proofs of purchase with fellow refunders. Many of them also contain such incidental points of interest as letters, recipes, and household items for sale.

Most newsletters are small operations, run off on mimeograph machines by housewives working out of their garages or basements, although a few of them are printed professionally. Some newsletters list only refunds, while others list only chances to "switch 'n' swap" forms and qualifiers. Many, like *Refundle Bundle*, combine both these services, and also include ads by subscribers who are looking for specific trades or purchases.

The listing of available refund offers is obviously a very important aspect of any refund publication. The single greatest advantage for the subscribing refunder, in terms of these offers, is that the editors of refund guides have access to much more information about current offers than individual refunders could possibly get on their own. Refunder Linda Foskett, author of a valuable little flyer called *Refunding*, estimates that refunders who do not use bulletins miss out on about 90 percent of the current offers.

Since newsletter editors are constantly canvassing the country for information about offers, they can put at the disposal of their subscribers a vast number of local as well as national opportunities. In any one issue of *Refundle Bundle,* for example, I may list over three hundred current offers, worth an average of $100 in cash refunds.

The "switch 'n' swap" aspect of newsletters is valuable, too. Say you have the required form for a Beech-Nut baby food offer, but your kids are all in junior high. Through a newsletter you can advertise for a trade, saying that you'll give your Beech-Nut form to anyone who can supply you with a form for an equivalent offer, one which you can more likely collect on.

Trading makes it possible for two parties to profit, rather than have both of them lose out on refunds because of a lack of one or another part needed to cash in. Refunders are almost universally fond of the swapping aspect of newsletters, and for that reason many newsletter editors, myself included, reserve a good deal of space each month for advertisement.

## Four Ways to Swap

Since swapping is so popular with us refunders, I want to expand a little on what is swapped, and how. What you need to know essentially is that there are several different kinds of swaps offered; their relative usefulness to you depends entirely on what you have (qualifiers, cash-offs, forms) and what someone else may have that you need.

Basically, there are four kinds of deals that newsletters commonly carry:

1. **Cash-off deals.** A subscriber will offer, say, 20- or 50-cents-off coupons in exchange either for other coupons or for a hard-to-get form or simply for a nominal handling fee. Getting coupons through a newsletter, of course, saves you a great deal of time hunting for and clipping those

magazine and newspaper ads. This is quite a common practice, and I for one have never heard of a refunder running into legal problems for charging a nominal handling fee to deliver coupons.

2. **Form exchanges.** Those hard-to-get forms are probably the most popular item of exchange in any refund publication. Some ads specify that the advertiser wants a particular form or forms, while others are open-ended, with the advertiser offering either a one-for-one exchange or a "potluck" assortment of forms for a specified amount of cash, coupons, or labels.

If you've read about a valuable refund but haven't been able to track down the required form, the back pages of a newsletter will usually give you what you're looking for faster than any other source.

3. **Qualifier exchanges.** Qualifiers, too, may be exchanged one-for-one or in potluck assortments for forms, coupons, or cash.

4. **Complete deals.** A complete deal (often called a *complete cash deal*) is an exchange between two subscribers of everything needed to be sent in for a particular refund offer: the necessary forms plus the necessary proofs of purchase. These deals are made dollar for dollar: that is, the subscriber who sends you a $3 package (qualifiers plus form) will expect another $3 package, or three $1 packages, in return.

As Carole Kratz points out in her book, the complete deal is one way of sidestepping the prevalent one-per-family rule. If you're a regular user of Green Giant, you're likely to have a thick pile of that brand's qualifiers, but because of the one-per-family rule, you'll be able to use only a certain number of them on any given refund offer. But you can multiply your earnings in such a case by offering a complete deal to someone who *never* buys Green Giant, and getting in return all the necessary material for a refund on something you never buy.

The one-per-family rule is still, technically speaking, being observed, and indirectly, such a deal makes a new potential customer familiar with a hitherto unknown product.

By now you will have gathered that, when it comes to swapping, refunders don't operate by any rigid standards of trade. Anything can be exchanged for anything else. The only real consideration is that the exchange must satisfy both parties. With regard to this, it's up to the newsletter editors, to some extent, to see to it that their subscribers deal fairly with each other. Subscribers who have been "burned" on a deal by not getting what they expected frequently write to us to complain, and most of us make it a point to exclude from further issues any advertisers who have delivered less than they promised.

That sums up the kinds of deals offered by newsletters. How much will access to these deals cost you?

Refund newsletters cost an average of about $1 a copy, or less than $10 a year for subscription. Some are as cheap as 50 cents each, while even the most expensive, relatively lavish ones won't cost you more than $1.50 a copy.

Considering that you can find hundreds of current offers in each issue, subscribing can be one of the least costly investments the wise shopper can make. Assume, for example, that a single issue costs you $1. Then assume you spend another $1 on an exchange ad (advertising rates generally run less than a nickel a word) and an additional 25 cents for a handling fee. That's a little over $2 in all. If, by using the newsletter, you track down even a half-dozen cash offers, the publication will have more than paid for itself by the end of the first subscription month.

And anyone who can't find a half-dozen good offers in an issue just isn't looking.

Moreover, many refund editors offer ways to further reduce the cost of their newsletters to the subscribers. One of these, which I use in my newsletter, is to offer free issues to subscribers who can send me notices of new or upcoming offers, or who get a friend to subscribe.

To give you a broader idea of how newsletters work, the following section describes my own publication, *Refundle Bundle*. Although not everything I have to say about it holds true for the other newsletters, it is a fairly typical example.


## *Refundle Bundle:* A Case History

I started *Refundle Bundle* on the proverbial shoestring back in the autumn of 1973.

At the time, both Steve and I were teaching, and we had also just purchased a new house—a move that made it imperative for us to cut financial corners and come up with ways to bolster our savings. We tried many things to ease the burden of the mortgage payments. One of the few things that we both agreed was worthwhile was that I take up refunding in earnest.

My first few weeks as a refunder, after my friend Jenny got me started toward that initial Del Monte check, were both hectic and exhilarating. For a time my entire consciousness seemed to have been revamped along the lines of what was to become my Supershopping System. I thought of little else. I planned whole menus around refunds—current and future ones—and I bought only products that I knew would sooner or later net me some money in my "extra savings bank."

My excitement proved infectious, and before long I had managed to interest several friends in the idea of us all getting into refunding together, as a way of consolidating our savings. If I were already realizing savings as a lone novice, I reasoned, why not see if cooperation with others couldn't lead to even greater dividends?

*Refundle Bundle* began, then, as a simple response to our mutual need for more information about refunding. Our idea was that several people helping each other look for offers were bound to turn up more than each of them could find alone.

When I started the newsletter, I didn't really expect to end up as the editor of a thirty-thousand-member subscription network. All I wanted to do was to make it easier for me and my friends—there were thirteen of us to begin with—to profit from the manufacturers' rebates.

The first issue, which came out in November 1973, had nine pages, mimeographed and stapled together by hand. It listed about 150 offers that required no forms, and about another fifty that did. The beginning subscription rate was $7 per year, with 75 cents as the single-copy price. I had no advertising in that first issue, although I did optimistically include a bordered box announcing that in future issues I would be happy to print subscribers' ads at the rate of 25 cents a line.

It was a modest but satisfying start.

Slowly, very slowly, we began to grow. One of the nicest things about the refunding network is that word-of-mouth advertising spreads the news about bulletins a lot faster than most editors imagine is possible. This was certainly the case with *Refundle Bundle*. I talked it up locally, and so did my friends, and I guess this must have had some effect, because by January 1974, the initial thirteen members had increased to a still tiny but respectable fifty.

By that summer, we had two hundred, and for the next two years, although we laid out just about all our subscription fees in printing and other costs, the venture continued to expand, and even began to acquire a certain aura of "success"—at least in terms of its usefulness for our family.

By 1976, the newsletter had ceased to be merely an enjoyable hobby that netted us some extra cash; it had become an income-producing business. In April of that year, when our first son was born, I resigned from my teaching

job, and *Refundle Bundle* became my major income-producing activity.

In less than three years, my shoppers' money-saving
scheme had paid off handsomely. Subscriptions were up
past a thousand, and I had started mailing the bulletin out
by second-class mail. The 1976 issues contained not only
the usual current cash offers but also occasional recipes
and dozens of ads offering to trade labels, cash-offs, and
forms. This "Switch 'n' Swap" feature has remained an integral part of the newsletter ever since.

The following year we began to mail first class, and also
added a feature that I consider one of the most enjoyable
aspects of the bulletin. This is a "Tidbits" section, where I
print small items of interest that are sent to me from my
subscribers around the country. They include comments
(both good and bad) about individual companies, notices
of expirations and refusals, and a grab bag of personal
notes that help to make the newsletter the friendly, varied
paper it is.

Many of my subscribers are recent joiners who became
interested in refunding after seeing me on one of the many
TV talk shows I have appeared on in the last couple of
years. Others have joined as a result of good old word-of-
mouth—still the best way for a newsletter to advertise. Still
others were subscribers to my friend Carole Kratz's bulletin, *Gold'n Refunds,* whom I "inherited" when it stopped
publishing in October 1978.

I live in New York State, and I have subscribers from as
far away as California, and as close as the house next door.
We all come from different backgrounds, naturally, but we
share a commitment to savings that makes us all enthusias-
tic members of the vast refunding "underground"—or, as
my friend Flo from upstate New York puts it, the refunding
"family."

The *Refundle Bundle* format has expanded a lot over the
years, although my basic dedication to savings is un-

changed. *Right now the newsletter includes the following elements:*

1. an alphabetical listing of available no-form offers, with the expiration dates noted in the margin

2. a listing of form-required offers, with a separate selection of Procter & Gamble offers—since P & G is, by general consent, the refunders' favorite company

3. the "Tidbits" section

4. the "Switch 'n' Swap" exchange ads section

5. a glossary of common refunders' abbreviations, to help the new subscriber read the ads more easily. (See "the Refunder's Dictionary" at the back of the book.)

6. where to write for forms

Most other newsletters have a similar format, although some list refund offers by expiration date rather than alphabetically, and many include a good deal more in the way of personal stories, recipes, homemakers' hints, and the like than I do. I guess you could say that *Refundle Bundle* (or *RB* as I call it) is an example of the "no-frills" newsletter rather than the "chitchat-spoken-here" variety. Both types, of course, have their defenders.

In addition, I offer my subscribers various ways of earning free copies, and most other publications have similar schemes. I'll give a free issue to anyone who recommends a friend as a subscriber, or who sends me the first notice of 1) a new no-form offer, 2) an expired offer listed in a current issue, or 3) an official refusal of an offer listed in a current issue.

The mutual advantage of these "freebies"—for both my subscribers and myself—is obvious. Winning an issue gives them a free shot at all the *RB* features, and getting any of the information that merits a free issue enables me to keep the newsletter up to date and accurate. Since we're all in this together, cooperation means bigger profits for everybody.

That's my success story. It may not be a Horatio Alger tale exactly, but to me, the development of *Refundle Bundle* has been immensely satisfying. Several years ago I was a housewife trying to find a good, simple system to save some money. Today I'm the publisher of a bulletin that reaches refunders 5,000 miles away, a bulletin that, I think I can safely say, has enabled hundreds of fellow shoppers make drastic cuts in their grocery bills.

The *RB* story is not unique. Just as my subscribers form a coast-to-coast network of friends, so, too, do the subscribers of the over sixty other refund publications now in operation nationwide. Together we form a kind of huge extended family—a mass movement of shoppers that might be likened to an active and growing underground.

## Joining the Refunding Underground

Fifty million Americans regularly clip coupons. One shopper in four relies on refunding to realize extra dividends from her shopping. And these figures are constantly on the rise. Refunding has ceased to be the pastime of a select contingent. It is being taken up by thousands of people who only a few years ago would have scoffed at it as "quirky" or "not worth the trouble."

When I went on the "Today" show in 1978 to explain my Supershopping System, we received over one hundred thousand calls and letters asking for more information. That will give you some idea of how rapidly interest in this easy and profitable savings method is growing. When I say we constitute almost a mass movement, a shoppers' underground, I'm not being merely fanciful: the figures more than bear me out.

There are differences, of course, between this underground and others, the principal one being that, since we are not in any way a subversive organization, we really don't *want* to be "underground." Refunders are a notoriously gregarious lot. We do not shy away from publicity. On the contrary, one of the things we enjoy most about belonging to the newsletter network is getting to talk to people all around the country. I have pen pals in half the states of the Union now, and ideally, I'd like to extend the *RB* family to include every shopper in the country!

You should know, though, that the companies that issue refunds look at us with some ambivalence. Even though they are constantly coming out with new offers, and even though they are almost always polite and helpful to us, they do tend to wonder about refunders in general and newsletter subscribers in particular.

This is because some of them have had unfortunate experiences with bulletins that were sloppy about checking their facts and as a result printed erroneous information about offers. I've spoken to several company representatives about this, and all of them say essentially the same thing:

"We stand behind our offers, and we like refunders as a rule, but such-and-such a newsletter printed the wrong information on our recent offer, and it's caused us a lot of trouble."

When a company receives the wrong qualifiers or a request for an expired refund, it has to refuse the cash offer, but spend the same amount of time and paperwork as if it were honoring the request. And refusals, however justified, do cause ill feelings.

You can avoid this problem by subscribing to a reliable bulletin, run by someone who checks up periodically on her information. Sometimes it's a little difficult to tell who is reliable and who is not, but if, for example, you receive three or four refusals in response to offers listed in one newsletter, it's a pretty good bet that the editor is not on top

**GREEN GIANT.** Box 21-553, Le Sueur, MN 56058 **$1.** Send 5 ingred. panels from GG "Boil In Bag" potatoes. **$1.** Send 3 ingred. panels from GG Potatoes with special sauce. Box 21-614.                                      **NED**

**HOWARD JOHNSON T-SHIRT OFFER.** Bedford, PA 15522. **T-SHIRT.** Send 7 flat lids from HJ ice cream carton. Size: 2, 4, 6, 8, 10, 12, 14, 16.                **NED**

**MAZOLA.** Box 5431, Hicksville, NY 11816. **$2.** Send any size or combination of 4 Mazola labels. **$1.** Box 5250. Send any size or combination of 4 Mazola Oil labels.                                                          **NED**

**MRS. SMITH'S PIE CO.** Box NB460, El Paso, TX 79977. **$1.** Send 2 end ingred. panels from Mrs. Smiths yogurt or light pie.
**75¢.** Send end ingred. panel from 1 Mrs. Smith's yogurt or light pie.                                    **March 31**

**POST TABLEWARE.** Box 4074. Kankakee, IL 60901. **5 piece tableware set.** Send any 6 Post tableware POP seals/set. Seals on: Grape Nuts, Post 40% Bran Flakes, Toasties, Grape-Nuts Flakes, or Fortified Oat Flakes.                                                    **Sept. 30**

**(SWIFT) BUTTERBALL HOLIDAY REFUND.** P.O. Box 2590, Maple Plain, MN 55348. Up to **$2.50.** Send 1 yellow Butterball oval and 1 red Swift's Premium circle from front of plastic Butterball Turkey bag. **$1** refund. Send 2 yellow Butterball ovals and 2 Swift's Premium circles from 2 fronts of two plastic Butterball Turkey bags. **$2.50** refund.                              **Jan. 31**

**BREYERS,** The All Natural Ice Cream. **$1** refund offer. P.O. Box NB820, El Paso, TX 79977. **$1.** Send 3 "pledge of purity" from half gallons.          **April 30**

**GENERAL MILLS, INC.** Box 198, Minneapolis, MN 55460. $1 for 4 box tops Nature Valley Granola Bars.
                                                          **April 30**

Figure 12: If you subscribe to a monthly newsletter, you will find dozens of offers like these: (These are only samples; many have expired so don't write for them.)

of things, and maybe you should hunt around for a new bulletin.

For more information about our shoppers' underground, write to me at _Refundle Bundle_, P.O. Box 141C, Centuck Station, Yonkers, N. Y. 10710.

Join us. And together we'll save even more.

# STEP FOUR: Joining the Movement

In a nutshell, here's how you can join the highly profitable "refunding underground":

1. Most serious refunders subscribe to one or more refunding newsletters (such as _Refundle Bundle_) that list hundreds of refund offers they could not spot on their own. Newsletters are also the best place to arrange exchanges of qualifiers, coupons, and forms.

2. Subscriptions generally run less than $10 a year. Since newsletters list hundreds of offers each month, you can easily make back the cost of a yearly subscription with the first issue.

3. The big companies seem to be ambivalent about the newsletter network, because some bulletin editors have printed erroneous information about their offers.

4. If you subscribe to a reliable bulletin, you won't have any trouble getting your money.

5. The refunding "movement" is a truly national phenomenon. Most bulletin subscribers, as a result of joining the movement, have made many friends around the country as well as money.

# 6/Getting
# on the
# Gravy Train

If I've given the impression up to now that refunders never think of anything but money, I'd like to correct it in this chapter.

Actually, money is only one of many benefits enjoyed by the devotees of Supershopping. Yes, it's the meat and potatoes of the System, but that System offers many bonuses in addition. The "gravy" of the Supershopping banquet includes such things as free samples of products, numerous coupon giveaways, and enough free merchandise—from toys to clothing to kitchen appliances—to keep your house looking like Christmas all year round.

Many refunders are so attracted to the idea of receiving such bonuses—refunders call them "premiums"—that they devote the bulk of their savings time to acquiring them; I know more than one refunder half of whose kitchen apparatus (dishes, utensils, dish towels, and a hundred odds and ends) has been paid for by the big food companies. Other refunders, while concentrating on cash rebates, find the occasional acquisition of premiums a good way to stock up on Christmas and birthday gifts; to them, premiums provide that extra something that makes refunding more than just a steady diet of cash. (I guess they get bored with all that money.)

In this chapter I'll be talking about Step Five of the Supershopping System—premiums and how to acquire them.

## "Absolutely Free"

It's amazing how many things in this country can be had for practically nothing. The old advertising catch phrase "absolutely free" may not have the ring of absolute truth about it, but when you start looking into supposedly free offers, you find that it's often not far off the mark. For a nominal handling fee and no proofs of purchase, you can acquire thousands of manufacturers' giveaways. And in many cases the companies don't even require the fee; they'll send you the item for literally nothing at all.

Mort Weisinger, for example, wrote a two-hundred-page book called *1001 Valuable Things You Can Get Free*, which lists freebies ranging from wall maps to recipe books, from food samples to toys, from career guides to how-to booklets. Weisinger's book has gone through ten revisions since it first came out in 1955, and each revision has included a host of items not included in the previous volumes. To judge from this book, you'd think that every manufacturer in the country is trying to give something away.

Manufacturers give things away for a good reason. They see their gifts both as a way of introducing themselves and their products to new customers, and as a means of building good public relations. To take just a few illustrations from the Weisinger book:

> The Toy Manufacturers of America offer a 16-page booklet entitled "The World of Children's Play and Toys," including a toy selection chart

Mead Johnson Laboratories are giving away a "Poison and Overdose First-Aid Chart"

W. J. Hagerty & Sons will send you a free sample of its silver polish just for the asking

The Vanilla Information Bureau, for a 25-cent handling fee, will send you a free vanilla bean.

These particular giveaways don't require qualifiers, although more lavish gifts will. All you have to do for these is send your name and address to the companies, and wait for the gifts to arrive.

Now, strictly speaking this is not part of my Supershopping System, since acquiring gifts in this way doesn't really depend on developing wise shopping habits, clipping coupons, sending in refunds, or joining the newsletter network. I mention the Weisinger book only to make you aware that countless manufacturers out there are just waiting to send you promotional gifts. Whether or not you are a Supershopper, you can cash in on these ubiquitous premiums. In most cases, all it takes is a postcard.

If you *are* a Supershopper, however, your opportunities for receiving premiums will be multiplied considerably, and the chances of getting really expensive, rather than just "token," gifts will increase as well.

The active refunder has excellent opportunities to acquire things for free, because once you start clipping forms and getting yourself on mailing lists, the companies will knock themselves out trying to be the first to send you information about discounted and "absolutely free" items.

One of the most common types of freebie is the free sample. Manufacturers are continually giving away free bottles of bleach, free boxes of cereal, and free tubes of toothpaste to introduce you to new products and to expand the markets for their established products.

They do this in several ways. Sometimes they simply canvass a neighborhood with actual samples of the product, in either a trial or a small size. At other times they prefer to catch you in the store, and will distribute the samples at a special table or from a special display. Generally, this kind of promotion is advertised in the front of the store with posters and banners.

More frequently, however, the companies give you coupons for samples rather than the samples themselves. I recently received in the mail a store coupon for a new dishwashing liquid that, according to the accompanying flyer, "actually improves dry, irritated detergent hands" while you do the dishes. I don't know if it works yet, but I'm certainly going to give it a try: even if it only cleans dishes, I'll be getting a 12-ounce bottle of the stuff for free.

The dishwashing liquid coupon was part of a home mailer. You can also find coupons for free products in all the places that you find coupons in general: newspapers, magazines, and the stores. Even if the offer is only for a trial size, you'll save something by getting it free, and the wise shopper keeps an eye out for these freebie tickets.

Look, too, for the offers that refunders call "two-for-one" deals. Frequently companies offer a free bottle of a detergent, for example, to anyone who can produce evidence of having bought one (or sometimes two) at the regular price. This is a way of getting you to buy the product in the first place, and of insuring your continued interest once you do.

"Two-for-one" offers require you to mail in a qualifier or cash register tape as a proof of purchase, so they are like refunds except that the dividend is merchandise rather than cash. In either case, what the companies are saying is, "Thanks for buying, and we hope you'll continue to do so."

You can find two-for-one offers also in newspapers and magazines, in the stores, and in home mailers. Refunding bulletins frequently list them as well.

Probably everybody, Supershopper or not, has gotten a free sample at one time. The free sample giveaway is one of the most obvious and widely advertised devices that the companies use to get us interested in their wares. But samples are by no means the only things that they offer us. The range of freebies offered as rewards for buying is enormous. If you really concentrated on it, you could probably get the companies to pay for practically everything in your house, aside from the bills and the furniture.

## Gathering a Houseful of Goodies

Last summer, my husband and I took our two sons to the beach a couple of times a month. Stuart, our oldest, would bring along his favorite Raggedy Andy doll and drag it behind him in a little red wagon. One day, as I watched him struggle through the sand, I had a funny revelation.

"Do you notice anything odd about Stuart's bathing suit?" I asked Steve.

"His bathing suit?" he mused. "I don't think so. What is it?"

"It's the only thing on him we paid for."

Steve frowned for a moment, perhaps suspecting that I had taken up shoplifting. Then he smiled.

"That's right," he agreed. "Everything else is a premium."

Now, I had known for years that refunding was saving us money, but I don't think until I saw Stuart that day, decked out in company gifts, that I fully realized how many benefits *aside* from money the System had given us. The swimsuit itself I had bought (on sale, of course), but Steve was right: everything else had been free.

Stuart's slippers, beach bag, towel, and hat were a special terry cloth swimwear set I had gotten for saving Glad bag qualifiers. His tee shirt was from Campbell's. Raggedy Andy was from Crest. And the Red Flyer wagon, which would have cost us $10 in the store, was from Viva paper towels.

I had to laugh, realizing that my child was a walking advertisement for the American supermarket, but there was a more serious side to the revelation. It made me see clearly that even a basically cash-oriented refunder like me could

almost dress her children head to toe for free, if she played
the premiums right.

I was curious just how many gifts I had accumulated in
five years of refunding, so that night I took an informal in-
ventory. To my pleasant surprise, I discovered that, without even concentrating on them, we had acquired over two
hundred free gifts, some of them quite valuable, simply because we were a refunding family. And this was in addition
to $1,500 a year in cash.

The range of gifts was large. In addition to the wagon
and the doll, we had gotten the kids numerous other goodies: a pail and shovel from Pampers, a hand puppet from
Nestlé, several excellent books from Tide, and a whole
shelf of Fisher-Price toys from Crest. For the backyard,
Glad had sent us a barbecue set, garden tools, and some
great heavy-duty gloves; Nabisco had chipped in a lovely
outdoor tablecloth. Inside, we had coffee mugs from four
or five different companies, a crock pot from Imperial margarine, a spacious kitchen canister from Bisquick, and a
handy "help-shelf" from Ajax to keep the cleansers out of
the way. Not to mention socks from Hydrox, a baseball
jacket from Aim, a donut-maker and a hamburger griller,
both from Ivory, and enough potholders, placemats, and
utensils to open up a kitchenware booth at the next county
fair.

That's only a sampling, mind you. If I were to list every
item we've received for free, it would take five pages. And
the value, since many of the gifts are worth $1 to $5, would
be well up in the hundreds of dollars.

Premium giveaways work on the same principle as refunds. You buy a product and save the qualifiers. The manufacturer announces (in a magazine, on a package, in a
mailer) that you can get a given premium by sending in a
specified number of qualifiers. You send them in, with an
order form, if it's required. Your order goes to a clearinghouse, and in a few weeks you are the owner of a new shirt,
tote bag, coffee mug, cigarette lighter, or toy.

Figure 13: Premium order forms often have alternative offers.

# Getting the Most out of Your Qualifiers

Some people have the idea that, since you "don't get something for nothing," you must have to buy shiploads of soap before you can accumulate enough qualifiers for a premium.

This is not really true. Sure, the very expensive gifts demand a significant number of proofs, but the smaller ones generally do not. Figure 13, for example, shows order forms for two recently expired premium offers that were advertised in the women's magazines. The free mug from Nescafé required only two Nescafé inner seals, while the Chex cooking calendar required eight POPs. Moreover, if you cared to spend a little money to cut your waiting time, you can see that these manufacturers gave you a "money-plus" option: you could get the mug for one seal and $1.50 in cash, the calendar for three POPs and 50 cents.

In other words, most premium offers do not require unreasonable amounts of buying. If they did, nobody would respond to the offers, and the manufacturers would be stuck with warehouses full of unwanted potholders. The only really large amount of qualifiers I've ever laid out for a premium was for an unusually valuable gift. It was the Dazey Donut Factory offered to users of Procter & Gamble soaps (Zest, Coast, Ivory, and Safeguard), and it required seventy wrappers. I had used Ivory for years, and since they hadn't had a cash refund in some time, the wrappers were just piling up in my shoe boxes. I found I had enough not only for the Donut Factory but also for a popcorn maker.

That's a lot of soap. But I doubt that we would be enjoying homemade donuts tonight if I hadn't saved the wrappers; the retail price of the "factory," I later discovered, was about $20.

Earning premiums makes you realize how many different, but complementary, ways Supershopping can help you. As I mentioned earlier, all the steps of my System lock together to form a whole. Think back, for example, to my purchase of those twenty tubes of Crest in Chapter 3. I've explained how buying on discount, using coupons, and cashing in on refunds could add up, with such a purchase, to a three-way savings: the refunder's own Triple Play. But Crest now has free offers for two coloring books; when I send in for them, using the qualifiers from some of those twenty tubes, I will have saved *four* ways. In the process, I will have acquired an item that will some day come in handy as a treat for Stuart or Mark.

## How to Play Santa All Year—for Free

For a refunder as basically cash-conscious as I am, premiums come as extras. They may be delightful, but I always look on them as welcome additions beyond the savings I'm really after. In a word, to me they're gravy.

To many refunders, though, they are far more important. Many of my refunding friends, confronted with the option of sending in for money or a gift, wouldn't hesitate for a minute before ordering the premium. Some of them, indeed, turn the gift-getting into the meat and potatoes of the System, and let the cash refunds act as the gravy.

People who concentrate on premiums often do so because at one point or another in the year, they need a lot of presents for relatives or friends. They may have large families, or they may simply want to cut down on Christmas or Chanukah or other holiday expenses by getting the companies to do some of their shopping.

I know several refunders who do most of their holiday shopping not in that last two hectic weeks before December 25, but on a gradual basis all year long. They simply send in for every free gift they can, whether they think they themselves can use it or not. By Thanksgiving they've accumulated a pretty fair-sized stock of premiums, many of which prove to be quite satisfactory either as stocking stuffers or as full-fledged gifts. One Maryland refunder I know gets half her yearly Christmas gifts free.

People sometimes ask me if it isn't troublesome or embarrassing using all those company "promo" items. A Florida woman we met last year was convinced that our children were eating foods they couldn't stand, wearing clothing they didn't like, and playing with toys they hated.

Yes, we wear, eat, and play with a lot of company giveaways. But we certainly don't do it under duress. The kids eat Cheerios because they like them, not because the company is offering a cash refund. They play with their Frisky Froggy and pocket camera because it's fun for them, not because they came, without charge, from Crest. We wear our Charmin and Smucker's and Campbell's tee shirts because, for the price we paid for them (nothing), they're the best tee shirt bargain in town. And they're as sturdy and attractive as any shirt you'd pay $5 for in a store.

As for being embarrassed: I'm not embarrassed to say I'm a Supershopper, and that I enjoy every minute of it. Why should anybody feel embarrassed about saving money?

## "Relatively Free"

Remember the Nescafé mugs I talked about a few pages back? You'll recall that they were being offered under either of two options. You could get them for qualifiers alone or you could pay a small cash fee and reduce the amount of qualifiers needed.

The first option is known as a straight premium arrangement. The second is something refunders call a "cash-plus" or "money-plus" deal.

When you consider that even many "absolutely free" deals ask you to send a nominal handling fee in order to get your premium, I guess you could say that a lot of these offers are really only "relatively free": technically they, too, are cash-plus offers. But refunders use the term "cash-plus" more precisely than that, to refer to deals that the company specifically requests a cash payment (not simply a "postage and handling charge") in addition to proofs of purchase. Money-plus offers like this are quite common, and—as we saw with the Chex and Nescafé offers—many straight premium arrangements also have a cash-plus option.

Personally, I've never been fond of paying out cash to get anything that's being advertised as a free gift. There are so many really free offers around that it seems almost a waste of money to actually pay for a premium. For this reason I've generally excluded cash-plus offers from the pages of Refundle Bundle, and asked that my subscribers, when they write to inform me of new offers, mention only those for which no money is required.

Every so often, however, a particularly good money-plus comes along, and I'll make an exception. This was the case with a recent offer from Tide for a Velcro dartboard. They wanted 50 cents plus two proofs of purchase, and since I had priced similar dartboards in the stores at between $3 and $4, this looked like an offer I didn't want to pass up. I not only gave it a mention in RB but also bought it for our family room.

Naturally there are other exceptions, and if you don't happen to be as biased as I am against paying out cash (remember, this is a book about cashing in), you'll probably order more cash-pluses than I do. You probably won't be sorry, either. Generally speaking, you needn't be worried with cash-pluses about buying a pig in a poke. The merchandise offered is almost always well worth the price being asked; and in many cases it's considerably below retail.

The Nescafé mugs, for example, were advertised for $1.50 each, plus an inner seal. I got them free, of course, but I can see that even at $1.50 they'd be a bargain. I haven't seen anything comparable in the stores for under $3.

Another type of promotion that offers "relatively free"

premiums is the *point coupon* system, whereby a shopper saves proofs of purchase, each one worth a designated number of "points," until he or she has accumulated enough points to "purchase" a desired gift from the manufacturer's catalog. The most famous, and oldest, point system in this country is the Betty Crocker coupon plan, which General Mills started back in 1930 to generate product loyalty. The General Mills catalog offers kitchenware and other items that the shopper can order either for points alone or for a combination of points and cash. You can order a copy of the current Betty Crocker catalog from General Mills, 400 Second Avenue South, Minneapolis, Minnesota 55440.

Many people swear by this plan, and I have nothing against it except that, as Carole Kratz points out in her book, when you're point couponing, you "tend to scatter your shot at cash refunding." That is, if you're diligently hoarding all General Mills's POPs with the catalog in mind, you're bound to miss out on the cash refunds that may become available between the time you begin saving your points and the time you have enough to cash in. For example, if there's a $1 refund on Betty Crocker cake mixes, you'll have to decide whether you want the money now or the premium later. There's no right decision, of course; it's a matter of personal preference.

The same thing applies to trading stamp programs. The companies that issue trading stamps (S & H, Blue Chip, and Top Value are the giants in the field) bank on you wanting the items in their catalog badly enough that you will be willing to shop exclusively at those stores that offer stamps, and ignore those without them—even though their prices may be lower.

I've seen some lovely gifts being offered by trading stamp companies, but I don't think there's any question that shoppers pay for their stamps in higher prices at the stores. The cost of trading stamps is simply passed on to the consumer at the checkout counter, and so you have to determine whether that alarm clock you've been eyeing is worth missing out on the sales and generally lower prices that exist in stores that do not feature stamps.

For me, it's not worth it. You'll remember I said in Chapter 2 that the Supershopper switches stores at will to follow the sales, coupons, and refund offers. You can't do that if you're obliged to buy only where stamps are offered.

The best way to earn premiums is to shop where the prices are best, to buy only name brands, and to faithfully clip every coupon, label, and refund form in sight. Shopping that way may have made me miss out on a few real bargains from Betty Crocker or S & H, but it's enabled me to fill my house with goodies—not to mention cash—from numerous other companies, and to purchase occasional money-plus items that would be cheap at twice the price.

Whether this system will be best for you I can't determine. For myself, I'm not complaining.

## Cash and Premiums by Mail

Nobody can live without money. Not in this country, anyway.

For that reason I've always considered the cash refund to be the cornerstone of my Supershopping System. I concentrate my efforts on getting those daily company checks, and I have to confess that the thing that pleases me most about the System is knowing that my refund money each year provides my family with an extra bank account on which we can draw to meet extraordinary expenses, or just indulge a whim.

But there's more to the System than money.

For some the real thrill of refunding has relatively little to do with either cashing in coupons at the checkout or opening the daily checks. For them the greatest satisfaction comes when they receive a manufacturer's bonus, so to speak, in the form of a valuable premium.

The proof of their success, therefore, lies in the many quality gifts to which their refunding has given them access. Whether they use these gifts for themselves or for others, it's acquiring merchandise for nothing that makes them feel that they're on the gravy train.

For most refunders, not surprisingly, Supershopping means a little bit of both benefits (or, better, a *lot* of both). I guess, in fact, that the most successful Supershoppers of all are those who see no firm distinction between a cash refund and a gift. These are the people who follow the Refunder's S.O.S. so religiously that they are always sending in for *something*. They have come to see the whole supermarketing system as a game they can win, and they view everything they get from the companies—monetary or material—as just fine.

These folks ride the gravy train all the time, because they have taken to heart something I've stressed throughout this book: that the System is an integral whole, all of whose steps work together. They are the Alert Shoppers, the coupon nuts, the avid refunders, the mainstays of the newsletter movement. They see Supershopping not as a series of unrelated gimmicks, but as an organized approach to the supermarket that can profitably restructure the way you shop and the way you save.

Gravy, or meat and potatoes? To the Supershopper, it's not really a choice. We want it all.

## STEP FIVE: Just Gravy

The final step in the Supershopping System takes advantage of the free gifts offered by the food and household goods corporations. The following pointers review how Step Five works.

1. Manufacturers, in order to induce you to buy their products, offer many incentives in addi-

tion to money. Called "premiums," these incentives include free samples, cents-off coupons, and free gifts.

2. Most premiums are between $2 and $4 in value. Some, however, are much more valuable. By saving qualifiers regularly, you can acquire, absolutely free, merchandise worth $10 to $20 or more.

3. The types of free gifts vary enormously. Among the most common offers are clothing, tools, small appliances, cookbooks, kitchen implements, and toys.

4. Some premiums are offered on a "cash-plus" or "money-plus" basis: the customer must send in money as well as qualifiers to get the gift. Even so, "cash-plus" premiums represent a great savings over the store price.

5. Most premiums are attractive, good quality merchandise. Because they make excellent gifts, many refunders think of "premium refunding" as a kind of year-round shopping spree; for others, it serves as a Christmas or Chanukah club.

6. Premiums can be your principal reason for refunding, or just gravy for the savings realized through the other steps of the Supershopping System.

# 7/Conceptions and Misconceptions

In the past few years I've appeared on radio and television programs from New York to California, and I've had to field hundreds of questions about my System.

No doubt many of these same questions occurred to you as you read the foregoing chapters. Although I hope I've answered some of them for you already, clarifying the less obvious aspects of Supershopping would probably be helpful at this point for even the most attentive reader. In addition, there are some issues I haven't touched on, which I'd like to clear up now.

The advantages of Supershopping seem almost self-evident to me. But I've been an active refunder and coupon clipper for over five years now, and I realize that people with less savings experience than I may be curious about elements of the System I haven't yet explained. To them—and to all of you who still have misgivings about Supershopping—I offer this chapter of questions and answers.

If you're skeptical about my System, I hope it will allay your doubts. If you're already convinced that we refunders are onto a good thing, I hope it will both act as a review and

tie up the loose ends you may have in your mind as to how
we go about it.

## Answers for Your Questions

I'll start with the questions I'm asked most often.

**Q.** You talk about Supershopping as if it has allowed
you to save almost incredible amounts of money. But
you're practically a professional refunder. What
about the rest of us? How much can we reasonably
expect to save?

**A.** You're right that I've become almost a professional refunder. I do devote a good deal of time to my
System, and I don't deny that it's my experience and
large back file of qualifiers that let me save as much as
80 or 90 percent on some shopping trips. But even the
novice refunder can realize very good savings, and
with a little effort *any* refunder can cut his or her
weekly bill by at least 20 or 30 percent. Carole Kratz
and Albert Lee, who wrote the book *Coupons, Refunds, Rebates,* claim that "earnest refunders can
save 50 percent of their shopping bill, and even a
modest effort will assure a 25 percent savings." I
don't think that claim is extravagant.

The amount of money you save by using my System
depends to a great extent on how rigorously you apply the principles of Supershopping to your own personal shopping habits. If you become alert to sales,
clip coupons faithfully, and get involved with refunding through the newsletter network, I see no reason why, within a very few months, you can't be saving just as much on your bills as I am: that is, about 50
percent every week.

**Q.** It sounds as if you live, eat, and breathe Super-shopping. Just how much time do you spend every week on the various parts of your System?

**A.** It's a common misconception that refunders spend their days clipping coupons and their nights dreaming about labels. I am a wife and the mother of two small children, and if attending to my System took that much time I couldn't have stuck with it for a week. I'd never have gotten anything else done.

I spend about five or six hours a week cutting coupons and forms, removing and sorting qualifiers, filing, and sending away for offers. That's a little less than an hour a day, and I try to make it seem like even less by doing most of my refunding work while I'm also doing something else, such as riding in the car or watching TV. A less organized refunder may end up spending a little more time, a more organized one a little less.

I know several people who spend more time than that each week on a hobby. And there are very few hobbies that regularly cut your grocery bill in half.

**Q.** I've seen a lot of cash-off coupons, but very few notices of available cash refunds. Where do you find all those offers?

**A.** Most shoppers are quite alert to coupons, but when it comes to refunds, they are blind. Part of becoming an Alert Shopper is becoming what I call "refund conscious." The offers are there, it's just a matter of attuning yourself to spot them, and then snatching up the form before they're all gone.

Refund offers appear in newspapers, magazines (especially the "women's magazines"), and home mailers. You can also find them in the stores on specially marked packages, on displays, and as hang tags. But by far the best source to locate these apparently elusive offers is a refunding bulletin or newsletter. The shopper who is really interested in tracking down manufacturers' rebates will subscribe to one or more of these publications, since their editors have access to far more refunding information than any single individual could have.

**Q.** I've never seen a refunding publication. Where can I get a copy of one, and how do I subscribe?

**A.** First of all, you can refer to the list of bulletins at the end of this book. You might also want to put up a small advertisement in your local supermarket, department store, or laundromat saying that you'd like to get in touch with refunders in your area, especially with newsletter subscribers. The refunding network is nationwide by now, and you should have no trouble getting responses.

You can also start by taking a look at my newsletter, *Refundle Bundle*. It lists about three hundred offers each month, and is available from P.O. Box 141C, Centuck Station, Yonkers, N.Y. 10710.

**Q.** Do you find more offers at certain times of the year than at others?

**A.** You don't really find more of them, but you do find different kinds, since some refunding offers are synchronized with seasonal shopping patterns. I've noticed a lot of refunds on ham around Easter time, candy around Halloween, and turkey at Thanksgiving. In the summer, Glad always offers free gifts (premiums) for use in the garden; we've gotten gloves, a barbecue set, and tools. At Christmas many of the big toy companies offer both refunds and premiums.

**Q.** Are there refunds on all kinds of products, or only new and exotic ones?

**A.** There are refunds on everything, and from time to time they repeat themselves, so the savvy refunder knows that getting $1 back this week on Del Monte tomatoes doesn't mean she should throw out all her Del Monte labels; they're sure to come in handy again. Every major manufacturer of food or household products offers refunds on a regular (if unpredictable) basis, and if you stick to buying only nationally advertised brands and save all the relevant qualifiers, you'll be sure to come in line for a refund before long.

Refunds are most frequently offered on paper goods, household aids, such as cleansers and detergents, and all kinds of processed foods: that is, items that have been boxed, frozen, or canned. You can't find very many offers for money back on unprocessed foods such as meat and produce, although there are occasional exceptions. The same thing applies to coupons.

**Q.** You talk about buying only nationally advertised brands. But it's obvious that store brands are cheaper than the national brands. Wouldn't I save more than you do by forgetting about your System and simply buying store brands?

**A.** No, you wouldn't. Store brands *do* have a cheaper face value, there's no denying that. But the trouble with buying them is that they are produced by smaller, independent manufacturers who simply cannot compete with the major firms in terms of shopping incentives, such as sales, coupons, and refunds.

Store brands generally run about 15 percent cheaper, on face value, than the nationals. But active couponing can cut your bill by 25 or 30 percent easily—and this isn't even counting the possibility of a future refund on that Kellogg box that you will never get on the store brand. Simple arithmetic will show you that Supershopping for the nationals can easily save you 10 percent right off the top over Normal Shopping for the "bargain" line.

If you don't practice refunding and couponing, of course, the store brands *are* cheaper than the nationals. But now you're talking about paying 85 cents for a store brand versus $1 for the known brand name. What Supershopping offers you is the opportunity to buy the same dollar value for as little as 50 cents.

**Q.** O.K., so you swear by national brand names. Which ones, in terms of your savings system, are the ones I should especially watch out for?

**A.** Coupons and refunds come not from individual products, but from the several giant firms that manufacture most of our processed food and goods. Therefore, what you really have to look for is not so much the trademark name but the big company that produced it and stands behind it. For example, you'll never get any money back from Jell-O per se. The people who will send you your Jell-O refund are at General Foods, the conglomerate that produces everything from Jell-O to Maxwell House coffee, from Minute Rice to Log Cabin syrups. Therefore, when you're focusing on refunds, look for the name of the manufacturer that will be printed on the package somewhere.

As far as which ones to look for, I pretty much agree with Carole Kratz's list of the Big Fourteen. They're reprinted here from her book *Coupons, Refunds, Rebates:*

| | |
|---|---|
| Best Foods | General Mills |
| Borden | Green Giant |
| Campbell's | Kraft Foods |
| French's | Lever Brothers |
| General Foods | Lipton |

| Pillsbury | Standard Brands |
|---|---|
| Procter & Gamble | Stokely–Van Camp |

In addition to these, refunders of course all have their own favorite companies and brand names. There seems to be almost universal agreement among refunders that Procter & Gamble is the best company around to deal with. Not only are they courteous and prompt, but they generally send you an extension of expiration date form when you send in for a nearly expired refund—and when you send for a form, they refund your postage! Close behind are General Foods and General Mills. In terms of individual names, I've also had very good experiences with Nestlé, Nabisco, Ragú, Kellogg's, Libby's, Marcal, Colgate–Palmolive, Johnson & Johnson, Borden, and Beech-Nut. (The addresses of many of these manufacturers can be found at the back of this book.)

This is not to suggest that other companies are not also both courteous and helpful. In over six years of refunding, I haven't run across more than two or three instances where manufacturers have been anything but cooperative. It's to their advantage, remember, to help you.

**Q.** Since you always shop with refunds in mind, don't you often find yourself buying things you don't need, just to get the refund?

**A.** I never buy a product I can't use just to get the refund. That would defeat the whole purpose of the System, which is to save money. Sometimes, however, I will go in for a "bulk buy," like my purchase of twenty tubes of Crest that I mentioned in Chapter 3. But I do this only in the case of staples or products that won't go bad sitting on the shelf. I will (and have) bought several cans of tomato sauce to cash in quickly on a refund that demands say, fifteen labels; but I

would never stock up on something like saffron—or
any perishable—because it would just end up going
to waste, and I would end up hating myself for being
gullible.

The essence of Supershopping is using the supermarket's offers to shop more sensibly than you do
now. I have a whole shelfful of labelless cans whose
labels have gone to make me money. (I know what
they are because I mark them with a Magic Marker.)
But I would not buy one item that I could not use.
That would merely be wasting space.

Not to mention money.

**Q.** Speaking of space, it seems that all those qualifiers you speak about would take up a lot of it. You
said you may have a thousand labels and box tops at
one time. Doesn't that threaten to force your family
out into the driveway?

**A.** Many people think that saving qualifiers takes a
lot of space. Veteran refunders know better. Many refunders work quite successfully even in mobile
homes. I keep my entire stock of proofs of purchase in
six shoe boxes out in my garage. That's a total investment of less than four square feet of space. I keep it
that small by keeping everything as flat and compact
as I can: flattening boxes, peeling off cardboard backings, and rubber-banding labels can help a great deal
in reducing the space you'll need for a working qualifier file.

**Q.** I've always kept my qualifiers spread out over the
kitchen counters, like a giant jigsaw puzzle. (It seems
to make them easier to spot.) How do you ever find
anything in a space just four feet square?

**A.** The jigsaw puzzle method is charming, I'll admit,
but it's not too efficient if you want to find something

quickly. I keep my qualifiers filed alphabetically in the shoe boxes, starting with Aunt Millie's spaghetti sauce and ending with Wesson Oil. It may seem like more work to begin with to set up a file like this, but, believe me, after a couple of weeks, it beats the jigsaw method every time. In the last couple of years I haven't had to search for more than two minutes for a single qualifier. And the more quickly you can find what you need, the more quickly you can pop it into an envelope and send away.

**Q.** You say you have over two hundred offers appearing in each issue of *Refundle Bundle*. Do you sit down in the middle of each month and just write away for all of them together? How often do you send away for refunds?

**A.** Holding it all off to do in one sitting makes your addressing seem like an impossible monthly chore. I try to avoid this by spreading my addressing over the month, doing a little each day and also doing it when I'm doing something else, such as watching TV. I try to send away for an average of one hundred refunds a month, so I'll be assured of getting back at least $100 a month in refunds.

You can save some time doing this by using rubber name stamps or labels for your return addresses. These are available from many mail-order houses. Imprint Products, 482 Sunrise Highway, Rockville Centre, N. Y. 11570, will send you one thousand labels for $1.

**Q.** With all that mailing, how much do you spend on postage?

**A.** Postage costs are inevitable in refunding, and they're difficult to reduce beyond a certain minimum. Since I send out about one hundred requests a month,

I spend about $15 a month on stamps. Envelopes (of course I buy the cheapest available, in bulk) come to perhaps $2 a month. I look at this expense as a kind of service fee to myself, and I take the cash for it directly out of my refunding money, so I won't feel the bite somewhere else. Considering that I'm getting back over $100 a month from the companies, I don't think it's an excessive expense. Another thing to note is that the cash I get back is kept in an interest-bearing account. That interest pays for the postage.

There are ways, moreover, to reduce it even further. Naturally, in any company correspondence where you can use a postcard instead of a letter, you should do so. That goes for correspondence with fellow newsletter readers, too. In newsletter exchanges, you should favor advertisers who include "EPOP—each pay own postage"—in their ads: that will let you split the postage costs with another refunder. If you're sending for several refunds from one company, put all the forms and qualifiers into one envelope rather than splitting them up into the individual offers. Companies I've found to honor this practice include Marcal, R. T. French Co., and Mrs. Paul's. You might include a note explaining what you're doing; I've never had a problem getting my refund when I do this.

You can also investigate the possibility of using third-class mail. This might be especially useful in trading large numbers of qualifiers or forms, as it can cut the postage cost of any mail over two ounces by as much as 30 percent. Check with local printers to see if you can purchase, at a discount, their mis-printed business envelopes. One woman recently purchased one thousand misprinted long envelopes for $4. "That is hard to beat," she says, and I agree.

**Q.** How long do you generally have to wait, after you send in for an offer, for your check to come back?

**A.** Most refund offers state that you should expect a four- to six-week wait for your check. This is a reliable estimate, but there are always cases in which it will take two or three months for the money to arrive. Don't get impatient, and don't write nasty letters to the companies. They have to deal with thousands of requests every month, and this frequently creates a backlog.

If you keep refunding records, you know exactly how long you've waited for a refund, and can act on that knowledge in writing to the companies. Most record-keeping refunders give the companies a couple of months grace period before sending out that "What's-happening?" letter; considering the backlog, that seems a fair approach.

It should go without saying that, when you do write, you should be polite and succinct. Just give your name and address, a description of the refund, and the date you sent in for it. Satirical comments about the company's tardiness may give you some perverse satisfaction, but they will not get your check to you any faster.

Since there's a less than 5 percent "no-show" rate for refund checks, many refunders, myself included, don't bother to check up on the companies. I'm sure I've waited months for some checks, and have sent in requests for some that never arrived. But the percentage of those is so low that, as long as I can keep getting at least $100 in the mail every month, I'm content.

**Q.** You say you receive about $1,500 a year in refund checks. Is this considered income, and do you have to pay taxes on it?

**A.** I certainly consider it income, but fortunately the Internal Revenue Service does not. Refunding is probably one of the few income-producing hobbies around on which you don't have to pay any taxes at all. The IRS looks at money sent to you for having bought certain brands not as income but as a reduction in the purchase price of the articles purchased. They make no distinction here between coupons and refund checks. So, all your refunding money is tax-free.

**Q.** I've heard that companies sometimes refuse to honor requests for their advertised refunds. Why is this?

**A.** Every refunder has at one time or another received one of the companies' "We-regret-to-inform-you" letters. This is nothing to get discouraged about. Companies refuse refunds for three main reasons. Either the customer has sent in for an expired refund offer, or has sent in for one not available in his or her area, or the request has been accompanied by the incorrect proofs of purchase. This causes disappointment, of course, but it's something that can easily be avoided if you read carefully the conditions of the refund (printed on the order form) before mailing in for it.

If an offer asks for the front panels from two 12-ounce-size boxes of A Rose Is a Rose detergent, for example, you can't send in one panel and expect to get your offer—even, in most cases, if that panel is from the 24-ounce size. Read the conditions carefully, and if you find that you were refused a refund because you sent the wrong qualifiers, send again, with the right ones. If you were refused because the offer had expired, chalk it up to experience and go on to other offers.

**Q.** I've been hearing a lot about "misredemption" recently. Is this the same thing as being refused an offer?

**A.** Not at all. Refunders are refused refunds because they have inadvertently failed to fulfill the requirements. Misredemption is a criminal activity practiced by people who are attempting to defraud the companies by submitting huge batches of cents-off coupons that have *never been used*, as is required, in the purchase of a product.

According to Jennifer Cross, author of *The Supermarket Trap*, misredemption is engaged in "by shoppers who take the coupon without the product, by stores who will give cash for *anything*, by counterfeiters, by thieves at the printers, and by promoters who clip coupons from discarded newspapers and stolen new ones." The last group is undeniably the most serious offender. It includes owners of stores who clip unredeemed coupons and send them in to the clearinghouses with bona fide redeemed ones; fly-by-night clearinghouses that similarly "salt" real coupons with fake ones; middlemen who pay unwitting charitable groups a nominal fee to collect coupons for them; and individuals who, posing as grocery store owners, redeem unused coupons that have ostensibly been redeemed at a nonexistent store.

It's not a small problem. The A. C. Nielsen Company, a major clearinghouse that has investigated misredemption over the past decade, came up with a list of seven thousand fictitious stores that were regularly receiving coupon reimbursements plus, of course, the handling fees. Since it is virtually impossible for even as large a clearinghouse such as Nielsen to check every supposed "store" in the country, there are obviously more sharpies out there still getting away with it. According to Ann Devroy and Ralph

Soda of the Gannett News Service, "Some industry sources say misredemption is reaching a level of $200 million a year." A cost that, incidentally, is immediately passed on to you and me, the consumer.

Luckily, some misredeemers have been caught. The United States postal authorities, working to beat this increasingly common type of mail fraud, recently issued their own fake coupon for a nonexistent new detergent called Breen. "When the dust had settled," say Devroy and Soda, "authorities found themselves with literally thousands of grocery stores trying to redeem coupons for a product that never existed." The owners of these "stores" were tracked down and indicted. In addition, the fake Breen coupons have been replaced with other, unannounced, come-ons; so perhaps the practice, which hurts us all as consumers, may soon be put to an end.

**Q.** I'm not planning to open up my own fictitious store, but are there any other illegalities I should watch out for?

**A.** Coupons and refunds are ways for the companies to get us to buy their products, and, strictly speaking, the only practices that are illegal in their use are those that try to get the advantages of the offer without paying the price: misredemption obviously fits this description. Beyond that you can do pretty much what you want. The *retailer* cannot "assign" or "transfer" the coupons redeemed to anyone else, but there seems to be nothing preventing you from doing so. That is, you can trade coupons, qualifiers, and forms as you please.

The one-per-family rule is something that many refunders ask me about. It is a hard and fast rule, but as I've indicated in Chapter 4, you can utilize the services of a newsletter. Remember that the companies are not out to trick you. If you can send them something that indicates that someone (not necessarily you) has bought the requisite number of boxes of their product, they'll usually be more than happy to send you your money.

Q. What do the companies think of your super savings?

A. In general, they don't mind at all. They issue coupons and refund offers, after all, as a kind of "reward" for buying their products—and refunders are not known as skimpers in that regard. Sometimes a company will get annoyed at a particular newsletter for printing the wrong information about an offer, since this creates problems when the subscribers try to cash in on it. But that is a small and infrequent problem. In general I've found the companies to be consistently helpful and in accord with what I'm doing.

Q. With the recent price increases for food, has your Supershopping System been growing in popularity?

A. Absolutely. When I started my newsletter *Refundle Bundle* in 1973, I had thirteen subscribers; today I have about thirty thousand. The editors of other refunding publications report similar rapid spurts in circulation. The inflation crunch of the 1970s has hit so many people so hard that they have had to adopt ways of dealing with the supermarket that would enable them to save without significantly altering their eating habits or the quality of the food they buy. Supershopping fits the bill.

Q. What advice can you give to those of us who are just getting started in Supershopping? What's the best way for us to realize the benefits of the System in the shortest possible time?

**A.** Probably the first thing you should do is to subscribe to a refunding newsletter; it will put you in contact with other shoppers in similar positions, and enable you to profit from the contacts and experience of the entire refunding community. Beyond that, the best advice I can give you is to open your eyes when you shop, to catch those sales and offers, to use coupons, and to follow the Refunder's S.O.S. outlined in Chapter 4: *save* everything, *organize* your savings system, and *send* regularly for your refunds.

There's no mystery about Supershopping. For me it's been the result of realizing that I'd save more by shopping intelligently than blindly; and of putting that realization into practice by taking advantage of the many manufacturers' offers that are available to anyone who has ever pushed a cart down a supermarket aisle. You can take advantage of them as easily as I have. All you have to do is to know that they are there, and then put in a modest amount of effort to insure that you get your slice of the Supershopping pie.

This book, I trust, will have given you a foundation on which to build your own Supershopping style. Perhaps, by adopting its precepts, you will come up with a system of cashing in that realizes even greater savings than my own. If so, I'd love to hear from you about it. One of the real joys of being a regular refunder is being able to exchange advice and ideas with shoppers all around the country. I hope, therefore, that you'll take this book not as a bible, but as a guide: something, in other words, that can help you bring out your own individual savings talents every time you go to the store.

In a sense, this book is an attempt to open the lines of communication between the hard-core refunders that are now saving so much on their bills and the vast untapped community of shoppers who want to save but who don't know how.

If you're one of that community, don't be shy. Drop me a line. Let's trade forms, labels, or ideas. Alone, we are helpless before inflation. Together we can all cash in.

# The Refunder's Dictionary

This glossary of abbreviations and terms is a compendium of those I use in *Refundle Bundle*, plus some from Lynda Foskett's useful Dover, Delaware, flyer, *Refunding*. Some editors may use other terms in addition to these, but this list will be plenty to get you started.

**CB:** Cardboard backing. The backing behind a pad of store forms, which generally gives an address to write to for a form, or for the refund itself, if all the forms are gone.

**C/D:** Complete deal, or complete cash deal. An exchange in which two refunders trade "packages" of all the material needed to cash in on a given refund: that is, forms plus proofs of purchase.

**C/O:** Cash-off coupon. Also called cents-off coupon. A certificate entitling the bearer to purchase a specified product at a reduced rate. Cash-offs are redeemed at the grocery store.

**Cpn:** Coupon. A cash-off generally available on

packages and in magazines, newspapers, and home mailers.

**CRT:** Cash register tape. Manufacturers occasionally ask for these as proofs of purchase in addition to the regular qualifiers.

**DM:** Direct Mailer. See HM.

**EPOP:** Each pay own postage. This indicates that each partner in an exchange is responsible for his or her own mailing costs.

**Form:** An order blank that must accompany the required qualifiers in certain cash refund offers. Forms are found in stores, magazines, newspapers, and home mailers.

**H/F:** Handling fee. Sometimes called a "shuffling fee." A nominal charge—usually 25 cents, sometimes 50 cents—required by some newsletter advertisers as reimbursement for sending out forms or qualifiers.

**HM:** Home mailer. Also called "direct mailer" (DM). A flyer or brochure sent to residences by manufacturers eager to interest potential customers in their products. Home mailers may contain coupons, free samples, or forms.

**HT:** Hang tag. A type of store form that is found hung around the neck of a bottle or jar.

**LSASE:** Long self-addressed stamped envelope. See SASE.

**LTD:** Limited offer. Indicates that the offer advertised is restricted to a particular area of the country.

**MF:** Magazine form. A refund order form found in a magazine.

**Money-plus:** An offer that requires that cash, in addition to qualifiers, accompany the request. Also called "cash-plus."

**NED:**    No expiration date. Indicates that the offer advertised has no prearranged closing date, and may therefore expire at any time.

**NF:**    Newspaper form. A refund order form found in a newspaper.

**POP:**    Proof of purchase. In one sense, this refers to the proof of purchase seals found on many products. It also means any qualifier, but the first meaning generally applies in newsletter listings.

**PP:**    Purchase price.

**Qualifier:**    Any part of a package that a manufacturer demands as a proof of purchase to accompany the request for a refund. Common qualifiers include box tops, labels, cash register tapes, and POP and UPC seals.

**REQ:**    Required, as in "required form."

**Round Robin:**    A trading system in which several refunders from different locations cooperate to exchange forms, labels, and coupons. Each member of the group removes what he or she needs from the circulating material, replaces it with equivalent items, and mails it on around the circle.

**SASE:**    Self-addressed stamped envelope. Many newsletter trades and sales request these to help defray mailing expenses. Some ads specify a long envelope, designated LSASE.

**SF:**    Store form. A refund order form found in a store.

**SMP:**    Specially marked package. A package that the manufacturer has indicated contains either a coupon or a form for a refund offer.

**UPC:**    Universal Product Code. A series of lines over a code number that appears on nearly all supermarket items. The UPC was intended to speed inventory-taking and to facilitate computerization at the checkout. Although the UPC system has not yet become fully effective, the codes are occasionally requested as qualifiers.

**1-4-1:** An exchange in which the traders swap forms or qualifiers on an equal basis, one item returned for each one given.

# Manufacturers' Addresses

Following is a list of some companies that send out forms upon request:

American Can Company
American Lane
Greenwich, Conn. 06830

Brown & Williamson Tobacco Corp.
Box 903
Louisville, Ky. 40201

Buitoni Foods Corp.
South Hackensack, N.J. 07606

Campbell's
Camden, N.J. 08101
Att: Consumer Service Dept.

Hunt-Wesson Foods, Inc.
1645 W. Valencia Drive
Fullerton, Calif. 92634

145

Johnson & Johnson
New Brunswick, N.J. 08903
Att: Baby Products Co.
or
Health Care Division

Lever Brothers
390 Park Avenue
New York, N.Y. 10022

Libby, McNeill & Libby
200 South Michigan Avenue
Chicago, Ill. 60604

Merrell-National Labs
Division of Richardson-Merrell
Cincinnati, Ohio 45215

Mobil Chemical Co.
Consumer Plastic Co.
Macedon, N.Y. 14502

Mrs. Smith's Pie Co.
South & Charlotte Streets
Pottstown, Penn. 19464

Pepperidge Farm, Inc.
Norwalk, Conn. 06856

Personal Products
Consumer Information Center
Milltown, N.J. 08850

Procter & Gamble
P. O. Box 432
Cincinnati, Ohio 45229

Vick Chemical Co.
Division of Richardson-Merrell
10 Westport Road
Wilton, Conn. 06897

Winter Garden, Inc.
Box 119
Bells, Tenn. 38006

# A List of Refunding Bulletins

Following is a sampling of refunder's publications. Where possible, I've indicated the name of the editor and the frequency of publication. Since advertising rates vary, they have not been included. If you write to a publication, indicate "Department CC" on the letter so they will know you found them through this book.

**Black Hills Saver**
Box 3075
Rapid City, SD 57709
Judith A. Biggin
Monthly

**The Clippers Bulletin**
Box 422
Argo, IL 60501
Barbara Michalik
Monthly

**The Coupon Clipper**
P.O. Box 1277
Pueblo, CO 81002
Cherie Carter
Monthly

**Croaker Clipper Bulletin**
P.O. Box 1721
Grants Pass, OR 97526
Millie Runyon
Bimonthly

**Ferolito's Refunder**
1521 N. Vassar
Fresno, CA 93704
Hertha Ferolito
Monthly

**Finder's Keepers/
   Gold Digger**
Box 36
Kinsman, OH 44428
Fran Verina
Monthly

**Firefly Reporter**
Box 263
Fulda, MN 58131
Isabella Neitch

**Gleanings**
218 DeWitt Avenue
Connellsville, PA 15425
Monthly

**Gold Mine**
Route 1, Box 75
Pukwana, SD 57370
Mary Graves
Monthly

**Growing Green**
P.O. Box 649
Cottage Grove, OR 97424
Roz & Jack Elligott
Monthly, except December

**Homemaker Ad Bulletin**
4411 Kelling
Houston, TX 77045
Maggie Lyons

**The Inflation Fighter**
Route 4, Box 161-F
Cleveland, TN 37311
Mary Younes

**Jaybee/Moneytree**
Valley Park, MO 63088
Claudine Moffatt
Monthly

**Jeanie's Corner**
Box 27044
Indianapolis, IN 46227
Jean Meador
Bimonthly

**Jeepers Kreepers**
  **Refund Peeper**
P.O. Box 1258
Thousand Oaks, CA 91360
Kitty Houghtaling

**Laura's Letter**
506 W. Elizabeth
Kirksville, MO 63501
Laura Mertz
Monthly

**Liberty**
Box 272
Concord, CA 94520
Kathleen Mero

**Mailbox Magic**
P.O. Box 32
Vienna, VA 22180
Bonnie Ragan
Monthly

**Merchandise Mart**
P.O. Box 202
Pleasantville, NY 10570
Betty Vogel
Quarterly

**Mini Bulletin**
259 Wembly Road
Upper Darby, PA 19082
Clarice Penna

**Money Back**
Route 3, Box 16AB
Grand Junction, MI 49056
Izola Meyers
Monthly

**Money Magician**
P.O. Box 53
Covert, MI 49043
Cathy Green
Monthly

**Money Maker**
Box 13564
St. Louis, MO 63138
Carol Backs
Monthly

**Money Talk**
181 Jackson
Edwardsville, PA 18704
Jean Kwiatkowski
Monthly

**No Form Needed
Round-Up**
Box 16
Hopwood, PA 15445
Rosemary Mehall/Mary
  Trimbath
Quarterly

**Quick Silver**
32 E. Main
Milford, NY 13807
Monthly

**Rainbow**
Route 1, Box 385
Ft. Orab, OH 45154
Dorothy Kattine
Monthly

**Realistic Refunding**
1296 Schuerman
Essexville, MI 48732
Judy Rivard

**Refund O Gram**
853 Geo. Wash. Hwy., So.
Chesapeake, VA 23323
Eugene F. Pettijohn
Monthly, except August

**The Refunder**
Box 883
Manhattan Beach,
  CA 90266
Sonja Winters
Eleven times a year

**Refunder's Ad Sheet**
2800 Hillcrest
Alton, IL 62002
Caren Caleme

**Refunder's Delight**
P.O. Box 547
Ferndale, WA 98248
Yvonne Oreb
Monthly, except August

**Refunder's News**
P.O. Box 388
Arvada, CO 80001
Linda Young
Monthly

**Refundle Bundle**
Box 141, Centuck Station
Yonkers, NY 10710
Sue & Steve Samtur
Monthly

**Road Runner Refunder**
5812 W. Elm
Phoenix, AZ 85031
Jan & Joe Neuberger
Monthly

**Saving with Sandy**
Route 1, Box 63-B
Poplarville, MS 39470
Sandy Lee
Monthly

**Score Card/Junk Magic**
7626 22nd Street
Sacramento, CA 95832
Maxine Cantrell/Gerry Lent
Monthly

**Shopper's Bonus**
P.O. Box 109
Marksville, LA 71351
Donna Caubarreaux
Monthly

**Your Refund News
Reporter/Extravanganza
Bulletin**
P.O. Box 12
Buffalo, NY 14226
Marian Iannello